The E-Policy Handbook

Designing and Implementing
Effective E-Mail, Internet, and
Software Policies

NANCY L. FLYNN

AMACOM

American Management Association
New York • Atlanta • Boston • Chicago • Kansas City • San Francisco • Washington, D.C.
Brussels • Mexico City • Tokyo • Toronto

This publication is designed to provide accurate and authoritative information in regard to the subject matter covered. It is sold with the understanding that the publisher is not engaged in rendering legal, accounting, or other professional service. If legal advice or other expert assistance is required, the services of a competent professional person should be sought.

Library of Congress Cataloging-in Publication Data

Flynn, Nancy 1956-
    The E-Policy handbook: designing and implementing effective E-mail,
Internet, and software policies / Nancy L. Flynn.
      p.   cm.
    Includes index.
    ISBN 0-8144-7091-2 (pbk.)
    1. Electronic mail systems—Management. 2. Information technology—
Management. 3. Computer network resources—Management 4. Computer
software—Management I. Title.
    HE7551 .F58 2000
      004'.068—dc21   00–060598
                                                                     CIP

Printing number

10 9 8 7

This book would not be possible without the generous gifts of time, encouragement, and support from my husband, Paul Schodorf, and our daughter, Bridget. As always, thank you.

Contents

Foreword

Think your organization is immune from e-risk? Think again. Misuse and abuse of corporate e-mail, Internet, and software assets can trigger costly litigation and protracted electronic nightmares that few employers are prepared to handle.

Take the case of the engineering firm that illegally installed, on *one hundred* company computers, a $5,000 CAD software program, along with a less expensive word processing package. Oblivious to federal copyright law, the firm loaded software with single-user licenses onto multiple computer workstations and congratulated themselves for their business savvy. They had maximized computer capabilities at minimal cost—or so they thought.

The firm's celebration came to an abrupt halt when a vengeful computer consultant, embroiled in a billing dispute with the engineers, reported the firm's software theft to the Software & Information Industry Association (SIIA) SPA Anti-Piracy division.

SIIA—which relies on informants' tips to police copyright infringement for software manufacturers—gave the engineers fifteen days to cooperate with a full-blown audit of all the firm's computer software or face multiple charges of computer piracy.

The potential financial impact? Tens of millions of dollars. Under federal copyright law, SIIA could recover the retail purchase price of all of the software the engineering firm should have bought, but did not. Alternatively, the SIIA could seek fines against the engineers of up to $150,000 for each item infringed. With two software programs illegally loaded onto 100 computers, the engineering firm faced potential fines of $30 million. Cha-ching!

The engineering firm sorely regretted its shortsighted decisions to copy software illegally and stiff a vendor. A five-figure, up-front investment in software (and payment of a mere $900 professional fee to the disgruntled consultant who reported them) could have saved the engineers an enormous amount of time, money, and embarrassment. In the end, the firm spent thousands of dollars on attorneys' fees and fines—which could have been avoided had the engineers put in place a written e-policy outlawing software piracy.

This story, based in fact, illustrates just how vulnerable many businesses are to electronic risks. A visit from the software police is just one of the e-dangers employers face. Any employer who grants employees access to the company's e-mail, Internet, or Intranet system faces a multitude of potential legal liabilities.

These e-risks, which are catalogued in this excellent book, include invasion of privacy, harassment, defamation, violation of copyright laws, and leakage of trade secrets.

In our law practice, we frequently advise business clients on the importance of drafting written policies to govern sexual harassment, employee violence, and other objectionable or illegal conduct in the workplace. Perhaps because of all the media attention these issues have received, most employers understand the role written policies play in protecting their organizations from liability.

Not so with e-policies. Many employers—including those whose businesses rely heavily on computer hardware and software—do not yet grasp the importance of establishing written e-policies to prohibit the unauthorized use or copying of software, and to regulate employee use of computers, e-mail, and the Internet.

In our opinion, no business that uses computers should be without written software, e-mail, and Internet policies. The implementation of written policies is one of the best ways to ensure your computer assets are used as intended for business purposes.

This book, *The E-Policy Handbook*, is the most comprehensive and helpful guide we know of to create these policies.

Although we have written many software and e-mail policies for our clients, we have gained valuable insights and suggestions from this book which we now have incorporated into our policies. Besides being packed full of valuable information, *The E-Policy Handbook* is a delight to read. We enthusiastically commend it to you.

Donald C. Slowik, Esq.
Christopher T. O'Shaughnessy, Esq.

Lane, Alton & Horst
Attorneys At Law
Columbus, Ohio

Preface

This book is designed to provide guidelines for developing and implementing effective e-mail, Internet, and software usage policies. It is sold with the understanding that the author and publisher are not engaged in rendering legal, insurance, risk management, computer security, or other professional services. You should obtain legal advice, insurance counsel, or other expert assistance as required from competent professionals.

Acknowledgments

Sincere thanks to all those who generously contributed expertise and information to help make this book possible.

Cyberinsurance experts: Assurex International's Thomas W. Harvey, Sharon Black, Kelli Black, and Rick Zesiger. Assurex Partners Andy Barrengos and Steve Sawyer of Woodruff-Sawyer; Brooke Hunter of Hunter Keilty Muntz & Beatty; Gary Kloehn of Barney and Barney; David Kohl of Roach Howard Smith & Hunter; Vernon O'Neal of Hamilton Dorsey Alston; Ronald Wanglin of Bolton & Co.

Cyberlaw and employment law experts: Attorneys Marie-Joëlle Khouzam of Carlile Patchen & Murphy; Dan Langin of INSURE trust.com; Mark Pomeroy of Bricker & Eckler LLP; Rita Risser of FairMeasures; Don Slowik and Christopher O'Shaughnessy of Lane, Alton & Horst; Joel Wesp of Teaford, Rich, Crites & Wesp.

E-risk management and computer security professionals: Joan Feldman of Computer Forensics Inc.™; Tom Flynn, coauthor of *Writing Effective E-Mail*; Steven Haase and William Corbitt of INSUREtrust.com; and Tami Pappas of CompuSleuth.

Software piracy information: The Software & Information Industry Association's SPA Anti-Piracy Division, with special thanks to Peter Beruk, vice president of anti-piracy programs.

I am grateful to Michael Crisp, publisher of Crisp Publications, for granting me permission to excerpt material from my book *Writing Effective E-Mail: Improving Your Electronic Communication*.

Thanks also to my friends and sounding boards Michael Cull and Bill Kistner, and to my assistant Lillian Moon Lee. Finally, a special thank you to my agent Sheree Bykofsky and editor Jacqueline Flynn for their belief in this book and help in making it happen.

PART **one**

Getting Started:

Assessing Your

Organization's

E-Risks

Introduction

Why Every Organization Needs E-Mail, Internet, and Software Usage Policies

"We'll be watching kiddy porn in the cafeteria at noon. Everyone's welcome."

Imagine that you are in the middle of the most important new-business meeting in your company's history when this disturbing e-mail message suddenly pops up on the computer screen of every employee in your facility. Making matters worse, this e-vil announcement is simultaneously broadcast as a voice message, reverberating from the multimedia workstation computers you've installed in every cubicle, each conference room, and all the executive suites in your building.

Your initial shock and embarrassment quickly turn to anger and concern as you come to grips with the fact that thanks to the tasteless joke of one out-of-control employee, you've probably lost a shot at this account and now are at risk of being sued by offended employees.

International Data Corp. estimates some 130 million U.S. workers send 2.8 billion e-mail messages a day.[1] Given that level of electronic activity, it is no surprise that e-mail has become more than the most common means of business communication. It has become the most risky, and potentially costly, as well.

Employee use of company computer resources, including e-mail, the Internet, and software, can open any organization, regardless of size or industry, to electronic risks. Among the most common e-risks are security breaches, malicious hacker attacks, lost productivity, wasted computer resources, e-viral infections, business interruption, and public embarrassment should a workplace lawsuit be filed, the software police drop by for a visit, or the media get wind of a particularly salacious e-disaster story.

In the Electronic Office, Risks Abound

It should come as no surprise to anyone with a personal computer and an e-mail address that employees are just as likely to receive offensive e-mail on the job as they are at home. In fact, according to an Elron Software survey, nearly 50 percent of employees with Internet access report receiving racist, sexist, pornographic, or otherwise inappropriate e-mail at work.[2] Some inappropriate messages are solicited. Other offending messages arrive unwanted and unappreciated. Regardless of how it finds its way into an employee's electronic mailbox, this type of message is a disaster waiting to happen.

With multimedia applications bringing sound and video images to more computer screens in growing numbers of organizations, the likelihood of employee exposure to offensive e-mail messages continues to grow. Simultaneously, the e-risks confronting employers are on the rise.

No Employer Is Immune from E-Risk

You cannot be present in every office on every floor of every facility every hour of every day. You cannot rely on managers and staff to exercise sound judgment and good taste 100 percent of the time. And you should not discount the damage external hackers and internal saboteurs can bring to your organization.

Should a female employee walk into the office of a male associate who at that moment is watching a pornographic video on his computer, you, the employer, could wind up on the wrong side of a sexual harassment lawsuit.

If a former employee subpoenas company e-mail in the course of a wrongful termination lawsuit, your organization could face a lengthy and expensive search for back-up tapes of e-mail messages. In one case, a Fortune 500 company was ordered by a court to turn over any e-mail that mentioned the name of a former employee who was suing the company for improper termination. With no policy in place for purging e-mail, the company faced the prospect of searching more than 20,000 backup tapes containing millions of messages, at a cost of $1000 per tape. The potential cost for that electronic search: $20 million.[3]

If your organization suffers a denial of service attack, overloading your network and preventing customers from making purchases or completing transactions online, you could experience lawsuits along with revenue losses and a lengthy period of business interruption.

If your employees are duplicating licensed software for illegal use by colleagues, friends, or family members, you could face six-figure fines, possible imprisonment, and searing negative publicity should the software police raid your company.

The list of potential e-disasters goes on and on.

Keeping Employees on Track While They Are Online

E-risks are as prevalent in the modern electronic office as e-mail is indispensable. For responsible organizations operating in the age of electronic communication, a written e-policy is an essential business tool. A computer policy that is well-written and effectively communicated to all employees is one of the best ways for employers to protect themselves from the risks associated with the inappropriate use of corporate software, e-mail, and Internet systems. It also offers some protection against attacks by malicious external hackers.

Among the costly problems a written e-policy can help protect against are productivity loss, workplace lawsuits, wasted talent, fines and imprisonment, public relations nightmares, security breaches, and wasted computer resources.

Lost Productivity

How much of the time your employees spend online is work-related? One hundred percent? Seventy-five percent? Fifty percent?

Do you even know? According to a Vault.com survey, fully 90 percent of the nation's workers admit to recreational surfing on the job. SurfWatch Software estimates nearly one-third of American workers' online time is spent on non-work-related pursuits. The type of sites with the greatest appeal to corporate cyberslackers, according to SurfWatch Checknet, are general news, 29.1 percent; investment, 22.5 percent; pornography, 9.7 percent; travel, 8.2 percent; entertainment, 6.6 percent; sports, 6.1 percent; shopping, 3.5 percent; and other, 14.3 percent.[4]

How bad is the problem? Firefighters in Columbus, Ohio, triggered an internal investigation, media sensation, and public uproar when a routine scan of on-the-job Internet surfing revealed that fire division headquarters' staff were visiting as many as 8000 pornographic sites a day.[5]

In 1999, Xerox fired more than 40 employees for idling away up to eight hours a day on pornographic sites. The downloading of porn videos was so pervasive, it actually choked Xerox's computer network and prevented employees from sending and receiving legitimate e-mail.[6]

Nationally, it is estimated businesses lost almost $500 million in workplace productivity in 1999, when Congress released the Starr Report and President Clinton's video deposition over the Internet. NetPartners Internet Solutions reports that some 13.5 million workers slacked off and logged on to see what the President, Monica Lewinsky, and independent counsel Kenneth Starr had to say about the relationship between the commander in chief and the intern.[7]

Workplace Lawsuits

The Internet contains explicit material that is potentially offensive to all employees—women and men, young and old, managers and staff. Reduce your e-risks by notifying employees that you will not tolerate the electronic sending, receiving, or viewing of offensive material.

As an employer, you could be charged with fostering a hostile workplace environment if supervisors, aware that employees are visiting adult-oriented sites, fail to discipline or terminate offending employees for their actions.

And it is not just the Internet that creates problems. E-mail also places employers at risk of litigation. When employees use company computer resources to send offensive internal or external e-mail messages, their actions can harm the entire organization. E-mail can be subject to discovery and subpoena in lawsuits, and old electronic messages can be admitted into evidence should a workplace lawsuit go to trial.

Employee misuse of corporate e-mail can result in six-figure litigation costs and million-dollar legal settlements. In one high-profile case, Chevron Corp. in 1995 was ordered to pay female employees $2.2 million to settle a sexual harassment lawsuit stemming from inappropriate e-mail circulated by male employees. The offenders' e-mail messages included, among other gems, "25 Reasons Beer Is Better Than Women."[8]

Wasted Talent

It is tough enough to hire, train, and retain talented employees without the added element of computer misuse and abuse. Inappropriate on-the-job e-mail, Internet, and software use can cost employees their professional reputations and jobs. It also can mean a sizable investment of time and money for employers who are forced to repeat the recruitment and training process.

The New York Times Co. learned this lesson when it fired 10 percent of its work force, nearly two dozen employees, and reprimanded another 20 workers for violating e-mail policy at the company's Norfolk, Virginia, Shared Services Center. As reported in *The Wall Street Journal*, most of the employees, terminated for sending and/or receiving e-mails that included sexual images and offensive jokes, were otherwise in good standing. In fact, one of the offenders recently had received a promotion and another had been named "employee of the quarter" prior to termination.[9] This is a prime example of bad e-mail decimating a good work force.

Fines and Imprisonment

In the United States, one out of every four business software applications is illegally copied, or pirated, resulting in $3.2 billion in lost revenue for software manufacturers.[10] Software piracy is a real issue, and both the federal government and the industry associations that police the problem take a tough stance against offenders. How tough a stance? One U.S. novelty and gift company, Oriental Trading, paid $525,000 to settle claims against it for operating unlicensed software on its systems.[11]

The fact that you are ignorant of software piracy laws or unaware of employees' use of illegally copied software will not protect you from prosecution. Get caught with pirated software in the workplace and you could face a lengthy period of business interruption, a $150,000 fine for each copyright infringed, a prison term of up to five years, public embarrassment, and negative publicity that paints your management team as unethical, tightfisted, and shortsighted.

Public Relations Nightmares

If you land on the wrong side of an employment practices lawsuit, you could find your company the subject of unflattering and unrelenting media coverage.

Allowing employees to go online to view sexually explicit materials, gamble, or engage in other inappropriate recreational activities while customers, vendors, and guests walk through your facility could cause you to lose credibility, reputation, and business.

Employ an executive who gets caught engaging in criminal activity online and you could lose the confidence of shareholders and the investment community, not to mention the patronage of customers and the goodwill of the public.

Hire just one individual with poor judgment or a lack of regard for your company's computer resources, and you could wind up e-mbarrassed and facing intense media scrutiny. Take the case of the Federal Communications Commission (FCC) employee who inadvertently sent a dirty joke entitled "Nuns in Heaven" to 6000 journalists and government officials. Instead of e-mailing the joke to his intended reader (a friend), the employee (responsible for mailing the FCC's *Daily Digest* to this same group of 6000) inadvertently sent the off-color joke to every reporter and decision-maker on the agency's group list. One employee's lapse in judgment and electronic mistake resulted in negative publicity and national embarrassment for the FCC.[12]

Security Breaches

Experts agree: Cybercrime is one of the Net's leading growth industries. Computer crime poses a major threat to U.S. businesses individually and the nation's economy as a whole. A review of the annual *CSI/FBI Computer Crime and Security Survey* is enough to convince anyone that cybercrime is growing almost as rapidly as our reliance on e-mail and the Internet.

Unauthorized use of computer systems increased in 2000, with 70 percent of respondents reporting breaches, as opposed to 42 percent in 1996.[13] All told, the FBI estimates computer losses at up to $10 billion a year.[14]

Wasted Computer Resources

If you think cyberslacking is harmless, think again. As reported by *Newsweek*, Lockheed Martin's e-mail system crashed for six hours after an employee sent 60,000 coworkers an e-mail about a national day of prayer, complete with a request for an electronic receipt. The defense contractor, which posts 40 million e-mails monthly, lost hundreds of thousands of dollars thanks to this one employee's action and the resulting system crash.

Before Lockheed Martin's e-crisis passed, a Microsoft rescue squad was flown in to repair the damage to the company's e-mail system and ensure this type of e-time bomb would never detonate again. The employee responsible for Lockheed Martin's e-disaster was fired for committing an act of sabotage.[15]

You may not be sending 480 million e-mails a year like Lockheed Martin is, but you no doubt have made a sizable investment in a computer system that is designed to enhance productivity and improve business communications. If your employees regularly make personal use of your computer assets, the return on your business investment will be compromised at best.

Take a Proactive Approach to Risk Prevention

The best advice for employers who want to reduce electronic risks in the workplace? Take the initiative. Don't wait for e-disaster to strike. Develop and implement written e-mail, Internet, and software policies now.

The E-Policy Handbook is intended to help employers of all sizes and industries navigate safely through cyberspace. The information contained in this book will help you identify your organization's e-risks, develop policies to mitigate your risks, and communicate and implement your policies in a manner that ensures employee compliance.

No workplace ever can be 100 percent safe from electronic risks. With the help of *The E-Policy Handbook*, however, employers can take big strides toward reducing risks, increasing productivity, and protecting corporate assets.

Forming Your E-Policy Team

Regardless of whether you operate a large organization with a full-time staff of in-house experts or a small business that relies on part-time help and the advice of paid consultants, you will want to form an e-policy team to oversee the development and implementation of e-mail, Internet, and software policies that respond to your organization's electronic needs and management challenges.

The size of your e-policy team will depend on the size of your organization, the scope of your electronic exposures, and your willingness to commit financial and human resources to e-risk management. For most organizations, the e-policy team will be made up of some or all of the following professionals.

Potential E-Policy Team Members

Senior Company Official

Increase the likelihood of e-policy success by appointing a senior executive to head up your e-policy team. The involvement of a top executive will signal to the staff that your company is fully committed to its e-policy program and expects employees to support the policies as well. With a white knight leading the charge, your e-policy team should have no trouble receiving the funding and support necessary to complete its assignment in a timely manner.

Research Consultant

You cannot hope to change staff behavior until you know precisely what type of computer-related activity your employees are engaged in. Merely assuming your employees are using your computer assets appropriately is not good enough. As a responsible employer, you must ascertain exactly how your employees are using, and perhaps abusing, their e-mail, Internet, and software privileges.

The most effective way to gather that intelligence is to conduct a comprehensive internal audit. An organization with a large staff and significant e-risks may want to retain a professional research consultant or other cyberexpert to customize a written e-mail, Internet, and software usage questionnaire, tabulate responses, and prepare a written report for the e-policy team's review. At smaller operations, the tasks of drafting the questionnaire, tallying responses, and preparing a summary report likely would fall to an e-policy team member who can be counted on for accuracy, sound judgment, and discretion. (See Chapter 2 for a sample e-mail, Internet, and software usage questionnaire.)

Human Resources Manager

Regardless of your industry or organization size, your human resources (HR) manager should play a key role in the development and implementation of your e-policies. Involve your HR manager in all aspects of the e-policy program, from planning, through writing, to training and enforcing.

If you don't have an in-house HR manager, assign the executive responsible for hiring, disciplining, and terminating employees a spot on your e-policy team.

Chief Information Officer

Your chief information officer (CIO) can help the e-policy team bridge the gap between people problems and technical solutions. Information management professionals can play an important role in identifying electronic risks and recommending the most effective software tools and techniques to help manage those risks.

Legal Counsel

No matter how well-written, comprehensive, and compelling you believe your e-policies are, do not circulate them to employees until they have undergone thorough review by an experienced employment law or cyberlaw expert. Have your legal counsel review your e-policies to ensure that all applicable federal and state laws and regulations are addressed and that rights are protected (see Chapter 3).

E-Risk Management Consultant

Effective electronic risk management calls for coupling management techniques and software tools. Have you educated your employees about your organization's risks and the ways they can help limit liabilities? Do you consistently delete e-mail messages that some day could come back to haunt you? Have you installed monitoring and filtering software? An e-risk management consultant can work with you to develop effective risk management guidelines to help structure and support your e-mail, Internet, and software usage policies.

Computer Security Expert

While developing your e-policies, take time to assess and address your organization's computer security concerns and capabilities. Computer security policies and procedures are designed to mitigate risks by keeping malicious external hackers and internal saboteurs out of your system. If your organization does not employ an in-house computer security professional or team, hire an outside consultant to assess and address your e-security risks (see Chapter 5).

Cyberinsurance Broker

No organization is completely free of electronic risk. Even with comprehensive, written e-policies in place, disaster will strike on occasion. Mitigate e-disaster liabilities and costs by putting into place a comprehensive cyberinsurance program. If you have not done so already, consult with an experienced cyberinsurance broker to review your e-risks and discuss the protection e-insurance offers (see Chapter 6).

Training Specialist

Your written e-policies are only as good as your employees' willingness to adhere to them. Spend as much time communicating your e-policies as you do developing them. Don't rely on employees to train themselves. Support initial e-policy training with continuing education tools and programs.

Make employee education the shared responsibility of your training manager, HR director, and the managers and supervisors who interact with employees daily and are positioned to correct inappropriate behavior on the spot.

Writing Coach

One of the most effective ways to control e-risks is to control e-content. An experienced corporate writing coach can help craft your written e-policies and develop a customized electronic writing policy for your organization. Your e-writing policy will work in tandem with your e-mail and Internet policies to ensure content is clean, clear, and compliant. Maximize the effectiveness of e-communication by having your writing coach take employees and executives through a refresher course on the ABCs and Ps and Qs of effective electronic writing (see Part 4).

Public Relations Manager

In the event of an electronic disaster—a hacker attack that shuts down operations, a high-profile lawsuit that captures the attention of the media, the arrest of an employee accused of soliciting sex from minors via the company's Internet system—your PR manager will play an important role in keeping employees, the media, customers, shareholders, and others informed, while killing rumors. Hope for the best, but plan for the worst. Incorporate a written e-crisis communications policy into your organization's comprehensive e-policy (see Chapter 19).

Chapter 1 Recap and E-Action Plan: Planning a Risk-Free Future

E-communication and e-commerce are here, and they are here to stay. Almost all organizations, regardless of size, type, or industry, operate e-mail systems to facilitate internal and external communication. Access to the Internet is a given in most offices. And there has been explosive growth in the number of companies that have established Web sites to dispense information and sell products and/or services. From start-up dot-coms to Fortune 500 companies, it seems as though everyone today is engaged in e-commerce and e-communication.

According to Forrester Research, business-to-business transactions over the Internet are expected to reach $1.3 trillion by 2003.[1] All that e-communication and e-commerce is not restricted to corporate giants. Even the smallest companies are getting into the act. A survey conducted by Bruskin-Goldring for Bank One reveals that almost half (49 percent) of small-business owners with 10 or fewer employees have Internet access. Among them, 35 percent operate their own Web sites.[2]

With all that electronic activity comes risk. Employee use of corporate computer resources can open an organization to liability risks, jeopardize security, and waste productivity.

Fortunately, employers do not have to sit by and wait for e-disaster to strike. By assessing employees' attitudes toward and use of computer assets, establishing proper e-risk management and security procedures, buying the right cyberinsurance products, and enforcing written e-policies, employers can take big strides toward reducing electronic risks in the workplace.

No organization—public or private, for-profit or not-for-profit, international giant or regional small business—can afford to engage in electronic communication and e-commerce unprepared. The potential risks and costs are too great.

1. Marshal the combined expertise of your e-policy team, and get to work on the timely development of written e-mail, Internet, and software usage policies.
2. While developing your e-policies, review related policies that can play a significant role in e-risk reduction. If your e-risk management, e-security, e-insurance, and e-writing policies are inadequate or nonexistent, now is the time to address them.

Conducting a Comprehensive E-Audit

Introduction: Uncovering Computer System Uses and Abuses

There is no such thing as a standard, one-size-fits-all e-policy. Corporate culture and employee computer capabilities combine with other factors to create within each organization a distinct environment with unique electronic risks and policy needs.

Before embarking on e-policy development, conduct an internal e-mail, Internet, and software usage audit to pinpoint your organization's specific e-risks and evaluate your employees' electronic capabilities.

A comprehensive e-audit will reveal how employees are using, misusing, and perhaps abusing the organization's computer system. It also will provide insights into what managers and supervisors currently are doing to monitor employee computer use and correct problems.

Your internal e-audit will enable you to identify your organization's electronic exposures and draft e-policies that specifically address those risks. In addition, your research will uncover any questions and concerns employees may have regarding appropriate and inappropriate online behavior. This information will facilitate development of a customized e-policy training program for your organization.

An effective e-audit should involve all employees. Senior executives and managers, full-time and part-time employees, independent contractors and freelancers, telecommuters and job sharers should all participate in your e-audit. Survey everyone who has access to your organization's e-mail and Internet systems. Question any employee who uses a home computer for business purposes, regardless of whether the computer is personal property or company-owned. Audit freelancers, subcontractors, and consultants who conduct business on your organization's behalf from computers located in their own offices and homes.

In the electronic office, risks abound. Use your e-audit to gather as much intelligence as possible about your exposures and your employees' computer use.

Host a Preliminary Planning Session with Managers

Before initiating your comprehensive, companywide audit, hold an e-policy planning meeting with managers, or perhaps a series of meetings. Confidential discussions with managers will give you greater insight into your organization's e-risks and e-policy needs, as perceived by the people who supervise and interact with the staff daily.

By involving managers early in e-policy planning, you increase your chances of winning their support for your e-mail, Internet, and software policies. Without the benefit of confidential, preaudit planning meetings, managers could be caught off guard by employees curious about or confused by the electronic communication audit and your proposed e-policies. Embarrass a manager today, and it is unlikely that individual will give your e-policies the attention and support they require tomorrow.

Following are some questions and discussion points you may want to explore with managers.

1. When it comes to employee use of the organization's e-mail system, what are the biggest or most frequent problems you see?

2. What about employee use of the Internet system? Have you noticed any problems or areas of concern there?

3. Do you perceive software piracy to be a problem within our organization?

4. What questions do employees most often ask regarding e-mail?

5. What questions do employees most often ask about Internet use?

6. What questions do employees most often ask about software use?

7. What do you consider to be the greatest electronic risks facing the organization?

8. What challenges do you anticipate the organization will face in the course of communicating and implementing written e-mail, Internet, and software usage policies?

9. Do you anticipate much employee resistance toward our new e-policies?

10. Are you comfortable assuming the role of an e-policy trainer and enforcer? If not, what is the source of your concern? What can the company do to increase your comfort level?

11. What questions or concerns do you have regarding the organization's electronic risks and proposed e-mail, Internet, and software usage policies?

How to Generate Staff Support for Your E-Audit

To maximize employee participation in the audit process and ensure honest responses, you must guarantee anonymity. Assure employees that management will make no attempt to identify respondents or penalize employees who, prior to the development and implementation of your written e-policies, may have misused the organization's computer system.

What follows is a sample memo informing employees of management's plan to develop comprehensive e-policies and encouraging participation in the e-audit. Along with explaining why the organization is developing e-policies, the memo ensures employees that their anonymity as survey respondents will be protected.

In addition, the memo clearly spells out for employees the benefits to be gained by completing the questionnaire. Because the memo comes from the company president, employees are alerted to the fact that the e-audit and the e-policies that will result from it are priorities for the organization.

Sample Memo

Date:	**April 20, 2001**
To:	**All Employees**
From:	**Matt Kennedy, President and CEO, XYZ Corporation**
Subject:	**E-Mail, Internet, and Software Usage Questionnaire**

Are you using the company's e-mail and Internet systems appropriately? While most employees are using the company's computer system for legitimate business purposes, we suspect some employees are making inappropriate or illegal use of our office computers.

While a certain amount of personal e-mail and Internet use is expected and authorized, we must control computer misuse. The inappropriate use of e-mail, the Internet, and software is a serious issue for XYZ Corporation and our employees. Computer misuse and abuse can lead to a wide range of costly problems. For the company, electronic risks include wasted productivity, business interruption, and workplace lawsuits. For individual employees, the risks associated with computer misuse and abuse range from disciplinary action to termination.

To help you and all employees make the most appropriate and effective use of online time, and to reduce the likelihood of costly electronic risks, we are planning to develop comprehensive e-mail, Internet, and software usage policies. When completed, these policies will spell out the ways you are, and are not, allowed to use the corporate computer system. Among other benefits, the policies will protect you from unwanted, disruptive, and embarrassing e-mails. In addition, the policies will make clear the penalties, including disciplinary action—and in some cases termination—violators will face.

As an initial step toward e-policy development, we are asking all employees, from entry-level staff to senior executives, to complete the following e-mail, Internet, and software usage questionnaire. The information gleaned from this survey will help us determine the specific e-risks our employees and the organization face, and will help guide us in the development of e-policies that are right for the company.

Absolute confidentiality is guaranteed. You have my word on that. We won't even ask your name.

Please answer all questions truthfully. Do not fear that an honest answer will land you in hot water. The company will not penalize you for inappropriate computer system use that may have taken place in the past. Our only concern is developing e-policies that will protect you and the organization from future e-mail, Internet, and software abuses.

After you have taken time to respond thoughtfully to this questionnaire, please drop it in the special e-questionnaire collection box we have set up outside the entrance to the employee cafeteria.   April 30 is the deadline for completion.

If you have concerns about this questionnaire, please give me a call at extension 110. I would be happy to sit down and discuss any questions you may have.

This questionnaire, and the comprehensive e-policies that will result from it, are important to the continued success of our company. Thank you for your help in making our e-policy initiative as successful as possible.

Sample E-Mail, Internet, and Software Usage Questionnaire

1. Have you ever used the organization's
   e-mail system for personal use?   ___**Yes** ___**No**

2. If the answer to question 1 is yes, please describe the
   type of personal use and how often you have engaged in
   it. (Please provide as much detail as possible. If you need
   more room, staple an additional sheet to this form.)

   _____

   _____

   _____

3. Have you ever used the organization's
   Internet system for personal use?   ___**Yes** ___**No**

4. If the answer to question 3 is yes, please describe the
   type of personal use and how often you have engaged in
   it. (Please provide as much detail as possible. If you need
   more room, staple an additional sheet to this form.)

   _____

   _____

   _____

5. Have you ever viewed or downloaded
   pornography via the organization's
   Internet system?   ___**Yes** ___**No**

6. If the answer to question 5 is yes, how often have you
   done so?
   ___**Once** ___**A few times** ___**Several times**
   ___**Regularly**

7. Have you ever participated in adults-
   only online chat during working hours? ___**Yes** ___**No**

8. If the answer to question 7 is yes, how often have you
   done so?
   ___**Once** ___**A few times** ___**Several times**
   ___**Regularly**

9. On a given workday, how much time do you spend reading and writing e-mail messages?

___0–14 minutes ___15–29 minutes ___30–59 minutes ___60 minutes or more

10. Approximately what percentage of the e-mail messages you send or receive are personal, totally unrelated to work?

___0% ___Fewer than 10% ___10–24% ___25–49% ___50% or more

11. On average, how many e-mail messages do you receive daily?

___0 ___1–9 ___10–24 ___25–49 ___50–99 ___100–199 ___200 or more

12. How much time do you devote each workday to personal, recreational online activity (gambling, shopping, chatting, visiting adults-only sites, etc.)? Be specific. Provide the type(s) of activity and the approximate amount of on-the-job time (in minutes or hours) you devote to it.

_____activity _____time

_____activity _____time

_____activity _____time

_____activity _____time

13. Have you ever received inappropriate e-mail messages at work? ___Yes ___No

14. If the answer to question 13 is yes, what type of inappropriate messages have you received?

___Racist ___Sexist ___Pornographic ___Otherwise offensive (please explain)

_____

_____

15. If the answer to question 13 is yes, did you report receipt of the inappropriate message(s) to your supervisor or a member of the management team? ___Yes ___No

16. If the answer to question 15 is no, why didn't you report the incident?

   _____

   _____

17. If the answer to question 15 is yes, what action did management take?

   _____

   _____

18. Have you ever sent an inappropriate e-mail message to another employee? ___Yes ___No

19. If the answer to question 18 is yes, what was the nature of the message(s)?
   ___**Racist** ___**Sexist** ___**Pornographic** ___**Otherwise offensive (please explain)**

   _____

   _____

20. Have you ever received an inappropriate e-mail message from another employee?   ___**Yes** ___**No**

21. If the answer to question 20 is yes, what was the nature of the message?
   ___**Racist** ___**Sexist** ___**Pornographic** ___**Otherwise offensive (please explain)**

   _____

   _____

22. Have you ever received a warning from management or been disciplined for sending or receiving personal e-mail messages?   ___**Yes** ___**No**

23. Have you ever received a warning from management or been disciplined

for spending too much time on the
Internet, engaged in personal business
or recreation? ___Yes ___No

24. Have you ever received a warning from
    management or been disciplined for
    spamming co-workers? ___Yes ___No

25. Have you ever received a warning from
    management or been disciplined for
    illegally copying software? ___Yes ___No

26. Have you ever received a warning from
    management or been disciplined for
    sending harassing, discriminatory, or
    otherwise offensive e-mail messages? ___Yes ___No

27. Have you ever received a warning from
    management or been disciplined for
    viewing, downloading, uploading, or
    disseminating pornography from the
    Internet? ___Yes ___No

28. Have you ever brought software from
    home into the office for business use? ___Yes ___No

29. Have you ever copied personal soft-
    ware for a colleague's business
    or personal use? ___Yes ___No

30. Have you ever copied one of the organi-
    zation's software programs for business
    or personal use? ___Yes ___No

31. Have you ever used the organization's
    computer to download software from
    the Internet for business or personal
    use? ___Yes ___No

32. Are you aware that it is illegal to copy
    licensed software? ___Yes ___No

33. To your knowledge, have you ever been
    given illegally copied software by a
    supervisor or co-worker? ___Yes ___No

34. Have you ever been instructed by a
manager to copy software? ___Yes ___No

35. Before sending an e-mail message,
do you take time to ensure that it is
well written and free of grammar,
punctuation, and spelling errors? ___Yes ___No

36. Once you delete an e-mail message, it is gone for good
and can never be retrieved.

___True ___False

37. If the company were sued, old e-mail messages could be
subpoenaed and admitted into evidence.

___True ___False

38. How do viruses enter computer systems?

a. Through e-mail attachments. ___Yes ___No

b. Via illegally duplicated, or pirated,
software. ___Yes ___No

c. Through software downloaded from
the Internet. ___Yes ___No

d. Through malicious hacker attacks. ___Yes ___No

e. All of the above. ___Yes ___No

39. The company has the right to read employee e-mail and
monitor Internet use.

___True ___False

40. Whom do personal e-mail messages that are written on
company time and sent via the company's e-mail system
belong to?

___The employee ___The company

41. Have you ever shared your computer
password with anyone inside the
organization? ___Yes ___No

42. If the answer to question 41 is yes, please explain the circumstances. (Do not use names.)

_____

_____

43. Have you ever shared your computer password with anyone outside the organization? ___Yes ___No

44. If the answer to question 43 is yes, please explain the circumstances.

_____

_____

45. Do you keep a written list of employee passwords? ___Yes ___No

46. If the answer to question 45 is yes, is the list in a secure location that only you can access, or is it readily accessible to others? ___Secure ___Accessible

47. It is a good idea to base your password on personal information, such as your date of birth, address, or social security number. ___True ___False

48. Do you ever leave your computer on and unattended? ___Yes ___No

49. Do you ever conduct business assignments on your home computer? ___Yes ___No

50. If the answer to question 49 is yes, does anyone other than you have access to your home computer? ___Yes ___No

If yes, who? _____

Chapter 2 Recap and E-Action Plan: Conducting a Comprehensive E-Audit

1. Involve managers early in the planning process to rally their support for your e-policy initiative and secure their commitment to enforce your e-policies.

2. Draft and conduct a comprehensive internal audit to assess your organization's electronic liabilities and your employees' computer capabilities.

3. Use the information gleaned from your management meetings and employee questionnaire to shape e-mail, Internet, and software policies that meet your organization's specific needs and risks.

4. To ensure the timely development and implementation of your e-policies, create an e-policy action plan, assigning specific roles and establishing a development and implementation timeline. The e-policy action plan that follows allocates one quarter, April 1 through June 30, for the sample company to form its policy team, hold planning meetings, draft a document, conduct a formal legal review, finalize written policies, and introduce the e-mail, Internet, and software policies to managers and employees. To save time, many activities take place simultaneously.

Sample E-Policy Action Plan

Action	Responsible Party	Completion Date
Team Formed	President	April 1
Manager Meetings	White Knight	April 10
Questionnaire Drafted	Writing Consultant	April 15
Questionnaire Approved and Distributed	HR Manager	April 20
E-Risk Management Assessment	Risk Consultant	April 20
Security Assessment	Security Consultant	April 20
E-Insurance Review	Cyberinsurance Broker	April 20
Questionnaires Completed	Employees	April 30
Questionnaires Tabulated	Researcher	May 7
Planning Meetings	E-Policy Team	May 10

E-Policies Drafted	E-Policy Team	May 20
Writing Policy Drafted	Writing Consultant	May 20
Crisis Policy Drafted	PR Manager	May 20
E-Policies Reviewed	Legal Counsel	May 30
Policies Finalized	Writer, HR Manager, White Knight, President	June 7
Managers Trained	HR Manager, White Knight	June 10
Staff Trained	E-Policy Team	June 30
Continuing Education	HR Manager, CIO, Training Manager	Ongoing

Timelines vary. An organization with a firm grip on its electronic exposures, an in-house team of experts committed to getting the job done in a timely manner, and a senior executive with a strong desire to defuse e-risks should be able to develop and introduce its e-policy program in less than a quarter. A company for which e-risks are new, and which must rely heavily on the services of outside consultants, may need a bit more time to put its e-policies into place.

Regardless of your proposed timeline, get a grip on your organization's e-risks, and go to work now on the development and implementation of written e-mail, Internet, and software usage policies.

PART two

Developing E-Risk

Management, E-Security,

and E-Insurance Policies

to Limit Liabilities

Cyberlaw Issues
Understanding Employee Rights and Employer Responsibilities

E-mail, Internet, and software usage policies may not be required by law, but they certainly can help keep your organization out of legal trouble. To date, employers have spent millions of dollars defending and settling lawsuits because of improper e-mail, Internet, and software use. And there is no end in sight.

In the not-too-distant past, electronic communication was not even an issue in the workplace. Today, employers are being hit with claims of sexual harassment, wrongful termination, discrimination, invasion of privacy, and copyright infringement—often related to inappropriate e-mail, Internet, and software use by employees. Some lawsuits are initiated by disgruntled employees and vengeful former employees. Other claims are made by customers, prospects, and strangers who happen to take offense at e-mail or Internet content. Still others are brought by the Justice Department and the industry trade associations that monitor software piracy.

While the federal and state laws and regulations governing e-mail, Internet, and software use continue to evolve, one fact remains clear: Organizations can help insulate themselves from many workplace claims by developing and implementing comprehensive, written e-policies.[1]

Talk with a Cyberlaw Expert

The sample e-policies and e-policy statements in this book are to
give employers general guidelines for developing e-policies. They
should not be implemented without consulting a local employment
law or cyberlaw expert. After you have drafted your e-mail, Internet,
and software usage policies, have your legal counsel review them for
accuracy and completeness. An experienced lawyer will be alert to
current federal laws governing e-mail, Internet, and software use, and
will be familiar with any state laws or regulations that may have an
impact on your organization's specific e-risks and e-policies.

Reconciling Privacy Expectations with Privacy Rights

Avoiding costly, time-consuming legal battles over e-mail and Internet
privacy is one of the best reasons to have a written e-policy. If your
employees are as poorly informed about electronic privacy as many
U.S. workers, they believe their e-mail and Internet activity is private
and that you have no legal right to look at their electronic communication.

Nothing could be further from the truth. According to the federal Electronic Communications Privacy Act (ECPA), an employer-
provided computer system is the property of the employer. As such,
the employer has the right to monitor all the e-mail traffic and Internet surfing on the company system.

Savvy employers appreciate the wisdom of monitoring e-mail and
Internet activity. According to the *2000 American Management Association Survey of Workplace Monitoring & Surveillance*, the number of
major U.S. firms checking employee e-mail and Internet activity is on
the rise. Since 1997, the number of employers who record and
review employee e-mail has more than doubled, up from 14.9 percent in 1997 to 38.1 percent in 2000. Over half (54.1 percent) of participating companies monitor employees' Internet use.[2] Clearly,
employers are growing more alert to the risks inherent in employees' online activity.

Stay Out of Court by Putting It in Writing

In spite of ECPA guidelines favoring the employer's right to monitor electronic communication, outraged employees have been known to sue employers for violating their right to privacy. In fact, there has been a 3000 percent increase in privacy lawsuits filed over the past decade.[3]

State laws, often more pro-employee than federal legislation, sometimes can be used to the employee's advantage. By demonstrating a reasonable expectation of privacy, an employee might convince a state court to rule against the employer's right to monitor e-mail and Internet use. The employee's claim could focus on the fact that since the employer had not read employee e-mail in the past, there was a valid expectation the employer would never do so. If your organization has reviewed e-mail only under certain circumstances, offended employees could argue that their cases do not fit those circumstances. Or, employees might claim your monitoring is particularly offensive.

If you want to avoid an invasion of privacy claim, the solution is simple. Use your written e-policies to give your employees explicit notice that they do not have a reasonable expectation of privacy. Notify employees in writing that you have the right to monitor anything that is transmitted or stored on the organization's e-mail and Internet systems, and that you intend to exercise that right.

With written policies in place, it is unlikely an invasion of privacy claim would take root. Minus written e-policies, however, you can find yourself embroiled in protracted and expensive litigation. The choice is yours.

Serve Notice before You Peek

The Electronic Communications Privacy Act permits the monitoring of employees' electronic communication under certain circumstances. Employers would be wise, however, to notify employees of the circumstances under which their e-mail will be monitored.

Use your e-policy to demonstrate respect for your employees and concern for your organization's future. Explain that only authorized persons will be allowed to review the staff's electronic activity.

Emphasize that you are monitoring e-mail and Internet use not to spy on individuals but to manage your organization's e-risks.

Educate your employees. Review the e-risks facing the company and the benefits everyone will enjoy if you reduce the organization's electronic exposures. Express your sincere desire to create a comfortable, harassment-free working environment for your employees. And ask your staff to help accomplish that goal.

Changes May Be Headed Your Way

Today, employers nationwide have complete control over company-provided computer equipment and service. That situation could change tomorrow. Should the laws governing electronic privacy be amended, the employer's right to monitor e-mail and Internet activity could be eliminated. That would place employers in the challenging position of maintaining harassment-free work environments without specific knowledge of the types of online behavior their employees are engaged in.

For the time being, however, employers can best protect themselves by implementing written e-policies and seeking experienced legal counsel. If you have operations in more than one state, it is particularly important to consult with your cyberlawyer. State laws vary, as do attitudes toward protecting employees' e-mail privacy and restricting employers' e-mail monitoring.

Sample Privacy Statement I

ABC Company uses a voice-mail system and supplies each employee with a voice-mail box for business use. ABC Company may access all voice mail at any time for any reason without notice to individual users. No one should expect voice-mail confidentiality or privacy vis-à-vis authorized Company personnel. The Network Administrator should be provided with access codes or passwords for use in such emergencies.

E-mail, the computer systems, and Internet also are to be used for Company business. E-mail is an efficient way to send urgent messages or those designed to reach multiple people simultaneously. Use extreme caution to ensure that the correct e-mail address is used for the intended recipient(s).

ABC Company may access and monitor e-mail at any time for any reason, without notice. You should not expect or treat e-mail as confidential or private. E-mail users must provide the Network Administrator with passwords. Except for authorized Company personnel, no one is permitted to access another person's e-mail without consent.[4]

Analysis

For employers who monitor both voice mail and e-mail, this privacy statement covers both issues thoroughly.

Sample Privacy Statement 2

Network and Internet access is provided as a tool for Company business. The Company reserves the right to monitor, inspect, copy, review, and store at any time and without prior notice any and all usage of the Network and the Internet access and any and all materials, files, information, software, communications, and other content transmitted, received, or stored in connection with this usage. All such information, content, and files shall be and remain the property of the Company, and you should not have any expectation of privacy regarding those materials. Network Administrators may review files and intercept communications for any reason, including but not limited to, for purposes of maintaining system integrity and ensuring that users are using the system consistently with this Policy.[5]

Analysis

The first sentence, "Network and Internet access is provided as a tool for Company business," sets the stage for what is to come and makes clear that the company monitors e-communication for business purposes. "You should not have any expectation of privacy," leaves employees with no doubt about their electronic rights or management's intention to monitor behavior.

Sample Privacy Statement 3

All information created, accessed, or stored using Company applications and systems is the property of the Company. Users do not have a right to privacy to any activity conducted using the Company's sys-tem. The Company can review, read, access or otherwise monitor all activities on the Company system or on any other system accessed by use of the Company system.[6]

Analysis
This statement also clarifies that employees have no right to privacy where the company's computer assets are involved.

Sample Privacy Statement 4
The Company monitors all Web sites visited. It is specifically prohib-ited for employees to knowingly visit sites that feature pornography, terrorism, espionage, theft, or drugs.[7]

Analysis
Here, employees learn not only that they will be watched but also the exact type of activity management is looking for.

There's No Place Like Home
In the event of a workplace lawsuit, employees' home computers may be reviewed along with the company's computers. You don't want to scare employees about the prospect of home computer invasion, but you do want to let them know that if their personal data is sharing space with company data, it might prove embarrassing in a lawsuit.

As part of your e-risk management efforts, you may want to pro-vide computers for employees' home use. Either maintain an inven-tory of notebook computers that employees can check out and carry home, or buy computers for installation at employees' homes.

Include full- and part-time employees, and consider providing home computers for subcontractors as well. If you retain the ser-vices of outside consultants and there is a subpoena, the consultants' computers also could be involved.

Talk with your employees. Stress that the computers you are providing are strictly for business purposes, not personal use. Dis-cuss risks. If there were a workplace lawsuit, a computer forensic expert would need access to computer drives, not just a few files. Whatever activity any employee in question might have engaged in would be open to review. If the computer were used strictly for business, there should be no problem. Otherwise, the employee and/or the employee's family could face considerable embarrassment, depending upon what showed up on the hard drive.

Sexual Harassment, Discrimination, and Defamation

One of the easiest ways to control risks is to control content. The establishment of an e-writing policy that clearly spells out the rules of netiquette and appropriate cyberlanguage will underscore the point that employees are expected to approach electronic communication in a businesslike manner. (For more on netiquette, see Chapter 9.) Appropriate, professional electronic communication means no racially or sexually oriented content, no harassing or menacing comments, no negative or defamatory remarks, no jokes, no ethnic slurs, no obscene language.

Use netiquette training to remind employees not to write messages they would be embarrassed to say aloud in front of customers, managers, or the media.

For added security, consider purchasing Employment Practices Liability Insurance (EPLI) to mitigate your financial losses should an employee ignore your policies and training and transmit an off-color joke, racially tinged comment, or sexually harassing message that ignites a workplace lawsuit (see Chapter 6 on cyberinsurance).

Sample Cyberlanguage Statement 1

All users must abide by rules of Network etiquette, which include being polite and using the Network and the Internet in a safe and legal manner. The Company or authorized Company officials will make a good faith judgment as to which materials, files, information, software, communications, and other content and activity are permitted and prohibited based on the following guidelines and under the particular circumstances. Among uses that are considered unacceptable and constitute a violation of this Policy are the following: (a) using, transmitting, receiving, or seeking inappropriate, offensive, swearing, vulgar, profane, suggestive, obscene, abusive, harassing, belligerent, threatening, defamatory (harming another's reputation by lies), or misleading language or materials; (b) revealing personal information such as your or another's home address, telephone number, or social security number; (c) making ethnic, sexual-preference, or gender-related slurs or jokes."[8]

Analysis
This statement leaves nothing to chance. Item b provides an added element of risk management, reminding employees that they are not to invade their co-workers' privacy.

Sample Cyberlanguage Statement 2
Users shall never harass, intimidate, threaten others, or engage in other illegal activity (including pornography, terrorism, espionage, theft, or drugs) by e-mail or other postings. All such instances should be reported to management for appropriate action. In addition to violating this Policy, such behavior also may violate other company policies or civil or criminal laws.[9]

Analysis
Here is a strong statement that drives home the point that in addition to keeping their online language clean, employees are expected to keep their electronic activity legal as well.

Copyright Concerns

While the laws and regulations governing e-mail and the Internet still are evolving, one thing is clear: Federal copyright law does extend to cyberspace. In fact, just about all the text, pictures, cartoons, art, music, videos, and software you encounter on the Internet are likely to be protected under U.S. copyright law.

Just as employees tend to be in the dark about online privacy expectations, so too are they generally ill-informed about copyright infringement. A marketing department employee who downloads clip art for inclusion in the company's e-mail newsletter could be in violation of federal copyright law. A department head who decides to stretch the budget by copying one licensed software program for the entire department's use is putting the company at risk of a copyright infringement claim and a visit from one of the national associations that monitor illegal software use (see Chapter 11). The training manager who types, verbatim, a few chapters of *Writing Effective E-Mail: Improving Your Electronic Communication* and e-mails the chapters to other employees has violated the copyright of coauthors Nancy Flynn and Tom Flynn.

As an employer, you are responsible for the on-the-job wrongs of your employees. Should an employee violate federal copyright law by pointing a mouse, clicking, and copying protected work, you could find yourself facing stiff fines, hefty attorneys' fees, and possible criminal liability.

Protect yourself through employee education and e-policy development. Make it clear to all employees, particularly in-house Web designers and communications/marketing professionals who have an ongoing need to produce documents and fill white space, that they are forbidden from downloading and using text, photographs, music, or other copyrighted material without permission of the copyright holder.

Sample Copyright Statement 1

Among uses that are considered unacceptable and constitute a violation of this Policy are downloading or transmitting copyrighted materials without permission from the owner of the copyright in those materials. Even if materials on the Network or the Internet are not marked with the copyright symbol, ©, you should assume that they are protected under copyright laws unless there is explicit permission on the materials to use them.[10]

Analysis

The incorporation of the copyright symbol, ©, is a good idea, since some employees may be unfamiliar with the symbol and its meaning. Equally effective is reminding employees that the absence of the symbol does not necessarily indicate the lack of a copyright.

Sample Copyright Statement 2

Users may not make copies of applications running on company systems for use at home, on laptops, or for other reasons without authorization. Users may not import, copy, or store copyrighted material without permission from the author. Doing so may violate application licensing agreements or copyright law.[11]

Analysis

This inclusive policy statement covers the illegal copying of software, as well as text and other copyrighted material. If you want to address software usage in your copyright statement, do so. But do not stop there. The illegal duplication and use of computer software is a worldwide, multibillion-dollar problem that deserves its own written policy and training program. Incorporate software education and a software usage policy as part of your comprehensive e-policy. (See Chapter 11.)

Trade Secrets

Theft of proprietary information may be the greatest threat to U.S. economic competitiveness in the global marketplace. According to the Computer Security Institute (CSI) and Federal Bureau of Investigation (FBI), the most serious computer-related financial losses have occurred by theft of proprietary information. Businesses participating in the *2000 CSI/FBI Computer Crime and Security Survey* reported losses of $66 million-plus from the theft of proprietary information, compared with $8.2 million reported lost to denial of service attacks.[12]

E-mail and the Internet make it easy for disgruntled employees and electronic intruders to steal trade secrets and confidential company information quickly and quietly.

Electronic communication also makes it easy for well-intentioned employees to slip up and accidentally e-mail sensitive company information to people who have no business reading it. All it takes is one typo or a single inadvertent click, and suddenly, confidential company information could pop up on the screens of dozens, hundreds, even thousands of readers. The accidental posting of a trade secret to the

Internet could cost an organization millions, possibly billions, in research and development dollars and time.

Whether it is your customer list, a secret formula, financial information, marketing plans, or a yet-to-be-unveiled advertising campaign, chances are your organization has information you want to keep out of the hands of competitors, the media, or other outsiders.

On a potentially more serious note, sending technical data to other countries may violate the U.S. government's federal export control laws. Your e-policy's trade secret statement puts employees on notice of the need to obtain management approvals (and an export license in some cases) before transmitting information to other countries.

Use your e-policy to drive home the point that company-owned secrets and proprietary company information should not be shared with readers outside the organization. Back up your policy with monitoring software. E-mail software that is programmed to detect key words will alert you if an employee addresses a message to a competitor, or if a member of the research and development team is discussing secret formulas online. (See Chapter 4 for more on monitoring software.)

Sample Trade Secret Statement I

Users must not use e-mail to send company proprietary or confidential information to any unauthorized person. Such information may be sent to authorized persons in encrypted files if sent over publicly accessible media such as the Internet or broadcast media such as wireless communication. Such information may be sent in unencrypted files only within the company system. Users are responsible for properly labeling such information, pursuant to the company's information protection policy.[13]

Analysis

While many employees will be familiar with the term *encryption*, not all will know what it means or how it applies to them. This statement, which clearly defines for employees what type of material needs to be encrypted and what is safe to send unencrypted would tie in nicely to your organization's e-training efforts.

Sample Trade Secret Statement 2

You may have access to confidential information of the Company, its associates, and clients of the Company. E-mail makes it very easy to send and receive information and attachments. It is also easy to send confidential e-mail to more than those you intended. If you have a business need to communicate confidential information within the Company, with permission of management, you may do so by e-mail, but only by sending the e-mail to those who have a need to know the information and marking it "CONFIDENTIAL." Company management may, from time to time, issue guidelines to those whose responsibilities include the internal e-mail communication of confidential information. Again, when in doubt, do not send it by e-mail. Memoranda and reports on paper, telephone calls, and face-to-face meetings should be used in some contexts, such as with respect to personnel matters.[14]

Analysis

This is a nice job of reminding employees that although quick and convenient, e-mail is not always the most appropriate way to communicate. Another plus is that the conversational tone of this statement makes a somewhat intimidating issue—trade secret violations—more accessible to employees.

Policy Enforcement

In some states, it is illegal to fire employees who have not been notified about the organization's expected standards of conduct. Your written e-policies solve that problem by putting employees on notice of exactly what the company expects in terms of e-mail, Internet, and software use. Gross violations of your written policies may, and should, result in immediate termination.

Sample Violation Statement 1

Your use of the Network and the Internet is a privilege, not a right. If you violate this Policy, at a minimum you will be subject to having your access to the Network and the Internet terminated, which the Company may refuse to reinstate for the remainder of your tenure in the Company. You breach this Policy not only by affirmatively violating the above provisions but also by failing to report any violations of this Policy by other users which come to your attention. Further, you violate this Policy if you permit another to use your account or password to access the Network or the Internet, including but not limited to someone whose access has been denied or terminated. If the person you allow to use your account violates this Policy using your account, it is considered to be the same as you violating this Policy. Both of you are then subject to the consequences of that violation. The Company may take other disciplinary action under Company policy. A violation of this Policy may also be a violation of the law and subject the user to investigation and criminal or civil prosecution.[15]

Analysis
This statement leaves employees no doubt about the organization's expected standard of conduct. E-policy violators should expect sure and swift disciplinary action.

Sign on the Dotted Line

Addressing the issue of privacy within your e-mail policy is one thing. Securing employees' consent to have their electronic messages read is another. Review your e-mail, Internet, and software policies with all employees. Then have every employee sign and date a copy of each policy to demonstrate that each employee accepts personal responsibility for adhering to the respective policies' rules.

Sample Personal Responsibility Statement 1
By accepting your account password and other information from the Company and accessing the Network or the Internet, you are agreeing not only to follow the rules in this Policy but also to report any misuse of access to the Network or the Internet to the person designated by the Company for this reporting. Misuse means any violations of this Policy or any other use that, while not included in this Policy, has the effect of harming another or another's property.[16]

Analysis
This effective statement solicits employees' support in policing the policy. Including a general statement that any action that harms another is considered a policy violation compels employees to exercise sound business judgment when composing messages and/or accessing the Internet.

Sample Personal Responsibility Statement 2
I,_____(print name)_____, hereby acknowledge that on this date I received a copy of the policy and procedure on Internet and e-mail access. I hereby acknowledge that I have read and understood the policy and procedure. I understand that if now or at any time in the future I do not understand this policy or procedure, or I have a question about it, or I believe there has been a violation of the policy, that I must contact my manager or any senior manager to resolve the situation. I agree to abide by this policy and specifically understand that violation of this policy may lead to discipline up to and including termination.[17]

Analysis
This personal responsibility statement does the job. It is clear and to the point.

Chapter 3 Recap and E-Action Plan: What Every Employer Needs to Know about Cyberlaw

1. For-profit businesses and not-for-profit entities can insulate themselves from many workplace claims by developing and implementing comprehensive, written e-mail, Internet, and software usage policies.

2. As an employer, you should inform your employees of the organization's privacy and monitoring policies.

3. Employers can control risks by controlling content. Incorporate cyberlanguage and netiquette guidelines into your written e-policies.

4. Educate employees about copyright infringement. Protect yourself by making it clear to employees that they are forbidden from downloading, uploading, or using text, photographs, music, art, or other copyrighted material without permission from the copyright holder.

5. Use your written e-policies to drive home the point that trade secrets and other company-owned information are not to be shared with unauthorized people.

6. Notify employees of the organization's expected standards of electronic behavior, and enforce policies consistently.

7. Require employees to sign and date copies of all e-policies to demonstrate their understanding of the policies and their acknowledgment that they accept personal responsibility for adhering to the policies.

8. After you have drafted your e-mail, Internet, and software policies, have your legal counsel review them for accuracy, completeness, and adherence to federal and state laws and regulations.

Developing an Effective E-Risk Management Policy

In the age of electronic communication, there simply is no way to guarantee a completely risk-free workplace. Employers can, however, limit their liability by developing and implementing comprehensive e-risk management programs that address document creation and content, document retention and deletion, e-policy enforcement, and employee privacy expectations.[1]

Establish a Policy Governing Document Creation and Content

At heart, e-mail is a communications tool that originally was intended for quick, informal communication. Where once we used the telephone to exchange business and personal information, today we use e-mail. And how. More people used the Internet in its first three years than used a telephone in its first 30 years.[2]

Unfortunately, by replacing informal phone chat with e-mail, we have created a process by which conversations are recorded and business decisions are documented electronically. The result is written ammunition that can make or break your case should a workplace lawsuit be filed.

In litigation over diet pills manufactured by American Home Products Corp., some of the most embarrassing evidence against the company came from internal e-mail exchanges among employees. In one particularly insensitive message reported in *The Wall Street Journal*, an American Home Products employee expressed her dismay at the thought of spending the balance of her career paying off "fat people who are a little afraid of some silly lung problem."

The employee's insensitive comment was an apparent reference to a rare, but often fatal, condition some diet-pill users developed. Inappropriate e-mail like this no doubt contributed to American Home Products' decision to settle the case in a deal valued at up to $3.75 billion, the largest settlement ever involving a drug company.[3]

In the past, if a lawyer were trying to uncover what employees were saying, doing, or thinking at a given time, the best evidence might come from notepad doodles, appointment calendar scrawl, telephone message receipts, and other informal documents. With the advent of the workstation computer and the prevalence of e-mail in the workplace, computer forensic experts today often have access to a library of written documents stored in electronic mailboxes and on hard drives, file servers, and backup tapes.

Thanks to e-mail, there is an unprecedented amount of documented business communication available today. An inappropriate e-mail message is not merely written, sent, and forgotten. In some cases, an offensive e-mail message takes on a life of its own, reproducing itself and traveling to dozens, hundreds, even thousands of screens in a matter of seconds. In the process, the writer runs the risk of offending growing numbers of readers and increasing the employer's liability concerns.

Give Your Employees Rules to Work By

To help reduce exposures and manage overall e-risks, responsible employers must establish and enforce policies governing employees' electronic writing. Settle for nothing less than good, clean commentary running through your employees' e-mail.

Good e-mail is businesslike and free of obscene, harassing, defamatory, or otherwise offensive language. Good e-mail is well-written and free from mechanical errors and structural problems. To ensure that your employees' electronic communication is as effective as possible, institute and enforce an electronic writing policy as part of your comprehensive e-policy (see Part 4). To guarantee that your employees' content is as appropriate as possible, be sure to incorporate cyberlanguage guidelines into your e-mail policy (see Chapter 15).

Sample Content Statement

Employees may not use ABC Corp's e-mail system, network, or Internet/Intranet access for offensive or harassing statements or language, including disparagement of others based on their race, color, religion, national origin, veteran status, ancestry, disability, age, sex, or sexual orientation.[4]

Analysis

This content statement leaves nothing to chance. Employees will have no trouble understanding what they are and are not allowed to write.

Establish a Document Retention and Deletion Policy

While originally intended to be a quick and convenient way to communicate, e-mail is being used more formally today. Contracts and other documents can be "electronically signed" over the Internet. Many organizations use e-mail to record business communications for posterity. Coupled with all that professional use, however, is an enormous amount of recreational activity.

Whether you like it or not, your employees probably are using the company e-mail system for decidedly unprofessional purposes. According to an AmericanGreetings.com survey, among adults who have e-mail, 76 percent report using it to send jokes, 75 percent make social plans via e-mail, 53 percent send online greeting cards, and 42 percent gossip electronically.[5] If your organization's e-mail retention policy calls for saving everything, do so with the under-standing that your critical electronic business documents likely are in bed with much more casual, potentially damaging e-mail messages.

Back in the precomputer days, space limitations forced most companies to purge their paper files periodically. Today, electronic files can be, and often are, saved indefinitely. That's a bad choice.

One of the most important components of a successful e-risk management program is an electronic document retention policy. If your company is like most, you probably don't have a formal policy for naming, archiving, or purging electronic files. Now is the time to put into place a document retention policy that spells out for employees how to categorize files, where to store files, and when and how to destroy files.

There Is No Good Reason to Save E-Mail Files

Backing up e-mail is equivalent to tape recording telephone conver-sations. There is no good reason to do so. There is, however, a com-pelling reason not to do so. If you are sued for some sort of work-place violation, every e-mail message that is backed up, both formal and informal documents, could be subject to review.

Are you using e-mail to document or memorialize business deci-sions? If so, those messages probably are intermingled with less for-mal, potentially damaging e-mail that could cost you your case. The best advice? Some experts say you should retain nothing. After all, what isn't there can't hurt you.

If You Must Retain E-Mail, Be Smart about It

Many employers who historically had saved all company e-mail have been jolted into action by the Microsoft antitrust case, the American Home Products trial, and other high-profile lawsuits in which old e-mail messages have played a damaging role in court. As a result, employers are becoming more cautious about e-mail retention. If you want to reduce liability but are uncomfortable with the idea of delet-ing all your organization's e-mail messages, strive for middle ground.

Some organizations, for example, opt to destroy e-mail backup routinely after 30 days. A month-long retention period enables the employer to retrieve data in the event of a crash. But because only a small number of stored documents are in the system awaiting review, exposure is limited.

The High Cost of E-Mail Retention

E-mail retention policies vary. An organization can back up e-mail on a daily, weekly, or monthly basis. To be safe, consider retaining e-mail for as brief a period as possible. The longer e-mail is retained, the greater—and more potentially costly—the risks.

According to the experts at Computer Forensics Inc.™, the average cost to restore and review one backup session for one representative day of the month is $30,000 to $50,000.[6] If, in the course of a workplace lawsuit, you were asked to produce a year's worth of representative days in which a particular employee was discussed, your cost would be $30,000 to $50,000 multiplied by twelve, if you were retaining e-mail yearly. That's $360,000 to $600,000 before you ever step in front of a jury. (A standard retention schedule typically is one backup session per month for a year, for a total of twelve monthly backup sessions.)

Had you not backed up your e-mail, your cost would have been limited to a review of what was on the system at the time the request was made. Obviously, it is much easier and less costly to open an electronic mailbox and read current e-mail than to go to a backup tape, build a server environment, restore the tape, open it, override passwords, and review the mail.

What's Your Excuse for Retaining E-Mail?

Given the risks inherent in retained e-mail, why do so many companies insist on backing up all their electronic correspondence? Some executives really do want to maintain a formal record of all business discussions and decisions. Others remain unaware of the risks associated with retaining both formal and informal electronic messages.

And at some companies, the information management professionals in charge of backing up data have not been educated about the legal exposures they are creating simply by doing their jobs.

Information management people typically are charged with ensuring that no matter what type of system crash or computer problem occurs, data is not lost and users can get back online quickly. Consequently, systems people tend to err on the side of overretention.

Employers who are sincere about reducing the risks of e-mail retention must educate their people, informing them fully of the e-risks facing the company. Once educated, technical personnel can help protect the company from risk, while still saving important data.

Sample Deletion Statement

All e-mail older than [thirty (30)] days will be automatically purged from mail queues and mail host backup. Users must explicitly save e-mail to user files when backup is required. E-mail should not be automatically saved, in order to reduce the need for system memory.[7]

Analysis

This statement may be too technical for the average employee to understand. If you want to use a comprehensive deletion statement like this one, be sure to combine it with training that covers "mail queues," "mail host backup," "user file," and other technical terms that may appear throughout your written e-policies.

As an alternative, you may elect to draft a basic deletion statement that all employees are likely to understand. For example, "The company automatically will delete all e-mail after thirty days. When backup is required, save documents to files. Do not save e-mail messages on your hard drive."

Force Employees to Empty Their Mailboxes

Do you know what your employees are storing in their electronic mailboxes? You may be surprised to learn some employees are saving e-mail messages from years gone by.

The problem is not merely electronic clutter. It is more serious than that. In case of a lawsuit, a forensic investigator first would ask for all the messages in your employees' active mailboxes. Next would come a request for backup tape. Finally, hard drives might be reviewed, if the forensic expert had reason to believe employees were storing information there.

An empty mailbox is a safe mailbox. Clean out overstuffed employee mailboxes with a combination of education and automation.

1. Reach out to your employees. Explain the organization's e-risks, and issue e-mail deletion guidelines individually. Tell employees you do not want them to hold onto old e-mail messages. Discourage employees from storing e-mail on their hard drives as an alternative to their mailboxes.

2. Explain to employees how the manual delete folder works. Many people do not realize that messages will sit in the delete folder forever unless the user takes steps to empty it.

3. Control whatever you can centrally and take advantage of new, more sophisticated management software as it becomes available. Assign limited e-mail space on your file server. Reduce the size of mailboxes; employees who tend to oversave mail will simply run out of room.

4. Install software that allows your e-mail systems administrator to empty employees' delete folders automatically every 30 days.

5. Be alert to the fact that your employees may be storing information on their hard drives to sidestep automatic deletion. Because no software exists to alert employers to the fact that employees are saving messages to the hard drive, education plays an important role. Make it clear to your employees that saving messages to the hard drive violates the organization's e-policy. Stress the fact that were the organization to be sued, all the material on employees' hard drives would be subject to legal review.

Limit Liability by Enforcing Risk Management Policies

Rely on your e-policy team (see Chapter 1) to ensure the successful implementation of your e-risk management policy and your comprehensive e-mail, Internet, and software policies. In particular, your human resources manager and chief information officer should play active roles in the introduction of your e-policies and ongoing employee education.

An effective e-risk management program should combine technological tools with people skills. Utilize all the e-risk management software at your disposal; then add a big dose of common sense to the mix.

Hush...Keep Your Password to Yourself

Would you buy an expensive luxury car, then leave it sitting unlocked in a public parking lot with the keys in the ignition? Doubtful. Do you go to sleep at night with all your doors and windows standing open and unlocked? Unlikely. Would you leave your purse or wallet sitting in plain view in a high-traffic, open-office environment? Surely not. Most of us go to great lengths to safeguard our personal property. Too bad we don't give the same consideration to our business assets.

In many offices, computers are treated casually, making it relatively easy for the unscrupulous to break in and steal data or funds. Use your organization's password procedures to lock out e-intruders.

1. Establish a policy of changing all passwords quarterly, sooner if a problem employee is terminated or other e-trouble occurs.

2. Maintain an updated record of employee passwords. Prevent employees from locking you out of your own computer system.

3. Use your e-policy to notify staff that passwords are the property of the organization, not the individual employee.

4. Instruct employees to store passwords in secure locations. It is not uncommon to find password lists taped to computer moni-

tors or sitting in employees' unlocked desk drawers. Common carelessness like this negates the purpose of security.

5. Prohibit the use of passwords that reflect personal information, such as an employee's name, birth date, social security number, or child's name. Instruct employees to create passwords that combine numbers, punctuation marks, and uppercase and lowercase letters.

Restrict Computer Access

While some organizations maintain tight physical security, controlling access to the building and monitoring movement throughout the facility, other companies exercise almost no control over visitors' activity. Likewise, effective e-risk management calls for the establishment of a few basic security measures.

1. Because it is tempting for co-workers, visitors, and hackers to walk up and use an open, online computer, instruct employees to shut off their computers if they plan to be away from their desks for more than an hour. If you prefer to automate, you can establish a password system at the workstation or network level. After a certain period of time, employees would have to use passwords to reenter unattended computers.

2. Authorize your chief information officer to establish policies that restrict remote access to your computers.

Investigate Unusual Behavior

If you notice or suspect out-of-the-ordinary employee behavior, have your information management people check it out. Systems professionals will know what you mean by "odd" behavior, and they can do a search to see if the employee in question has been dialing into the network in the middle of the night, downloading a large number of files, or engaging otherwise in suspicious activity.

In addition to investigatng isolated incidents, take steps to stifle employee urges to misbehave.

1. Have your CIO conduct periodic reviews to ensure that employees are not attaching unauthorized storage devices to their computers.

2. Look for clues. If an employee brings a large, removable drive to work, find out what's up. Oversized removable drives are used to download really large files. Ignore the obvious and you may facilitate the theft of valuable company data by an employee who is going into business or joining a competitor.

   Similarly, if you see an employee walking in with a new box of floppy disks or the like, there may be a problem looming. An employee who wants to remove a lot of information in a hurry likely would bring in a removable storage device or a big stack of floppy diskettes. These devices usually work faster than an Internet transfer.

3. Conduct routine audits. It is a good idea to conduct random audits of user e-mail on an annual basis, if not more frequently. If your random review uncovers a problem, such as inappropriate language or extensive personal use of the system, you have the option of developing and enforcing stricter e-mail and Internet policies for the entire organization or dealing directly with the individual offender.

Use Monitoring Software to Catch Bad Electronic Behavior

As an employer, you are obligated to create a harassment-free, discrimination-free work environment. You must control sexual harassment. You must prohibit the on-the-job collection and distribution of pornography. And you must prevent the use of e-mail as a tool to create an intolerable work environment. Many employers find control is best achieved by monitoring employee e-mail and Internet transmissions.

Don't leave e-risk management to chance. Install monitoring software to review and report on employee e-mail use. Software that flags key words, such as the names of supervisors, competitors, products, and trade secrets, will help you stay one step ahead of employees who may be preparing to grab sensitive information and run. When an "alert" word is used in an employee's e-mail message, the document automatically will be transmitted to a supervisor.

Employers who want to know what employees are thinking as well as writing are turning to a new type of surveillance software that covertly monitors and records every keystroke an employee makes. Let's say a disgruntled employee composed a nasty limerick about the boss, or a frustrated sales executive drafted a go-to-hell memo to a customer. Until now, employees could take comfort in knowing that once they regained composure and hit "delete," their ugly messages would disappear. Employees working in offices with keystroke loggers no longer have that safety net.

With keystroke logger software, all employee keystrokes are stored on the company's hard drive or sent via e-mail to a system administrator to retrieve as necessary. Every letter, every sentence, every comma, every typo, every revision is recorded. The employee's thought process and rough drafts are as accessible to the company as the final product is.[8]

Why would you want to monitor every draft, typos and all? As a deterrent. If employees know you really can read every word they write, they most likely will comply with your directives to use the company's e-mail system strictly for business, and in compliance with your content and cyberlanguage guidelines.

Similarly, your employees probably would be less inclined to surf inappropriate Web sites if they knew their workstation computers were data magnets. If you want to know what your employees have been up to on the Internet, all you need to do is look at their hard drives. Review the most obvious spots first. Pull down the list of sites most recently visited and any favorite sites that have been bookmarked.

Most Internet browsers store a list of sites visited, and some even store actual screen images. Employees who think they are visiting adults-only Web sites secretly may be surprised to learn the boss has the ability to call up and view exact replicas of the naughty pictures the cyberslackers have been looking at on company time. On a network level, software is available to enable network administrators to keep tabs on employees' online activity.

Sample E-Risk Management Policy

See Appendix B for a sample e-risk management policy, including guidelines for employees to follow in the event of a subpoena stemming from a workplace lawsuit.

Chapter 4 Recap and E-Action Plan: Putting E-Risk Management to Work

1. Control e-risks by controlling e-content. Establish and enforce policies that govern the creation and content of e-mail and Internet documents.

2. Consult with your cyberlawyer to determine the best e-mail retention and deletion policy for your company; then implement it consistently. Include an empty mailbox policy for employees.

   Remember, though, it is illegal to begin a document destruction campaign if pending litigation would be affected by it. So put your retention and deletion policies into place before trouble strikes.

3. Educate your employees. Provide managers and staff with e-scenarios that could affect the well-being of the company and the security of employees' jobs. Follow up with actions employees can take to help limit risks.

4. Keep your eyes open to unusual or suspicious behavior on the part of employees and outsiders. The adage "better safe than sorry" is never more true than when applied to e-risks.

5. Don't leave e-risk management to chance. Install monitoring and filtering software to control employees' e-mail and Internet activity.

A Computer Security Policy to Reduce External Risks

How vulnerable is your computer system to penetration by outsiders or unauthorized access by insiders? If your organization is like most, you are at ever-increasing risk of attack and financial loss. Seventy percent of companies surveyed by the Computer Security Institute (CSI) and Federal Bureau of Investigation (FBI) reported computer security breaches in 2000.[1] Among recent anonymous cybercrimes reported are the following:

- A financial institution with 5000-plus employees experienced a $1 million loss from the theft of proprietary information.

- A financial institution with a 10,000-person work force lost $1 million to data sabotage, $1 million to financial fraud, and $1 million to insider Net abuse.

- A $500 million high-tech company suffered a $500,000 loss when its system was penetrated.

- A petroleum and chemical company employing 1000 lost $1 million following a denial of service attack and another $100,000 when a virus contaminated the system.

- A $1 billion manufacturer reported a $1 million loss to financial fraud.[2]

Overall, cybercrimes are on the rise. A few specific examples from the FBI and CSI include these following:

- System penetration by outsiders increased to 25 percent in 1999, up 5 percent since 1997.

- Unauthorized access by insiders rose 16 percent between 1999 and 2000, up to 71 percent.

- Twenty percent of respondents reported theft of proprietary information in 2000, versus 18 percent in 1998.

- Denial of service attacks, which can gum up Web sites for hours, rose to 27 percent in 2000, compared with 24 percent in 1998.

- Sabotage of data or networks was cited by 17 percent of respondents in 2000, up from 13 percent the previous year.

- Insider abuse of Net access rose 11 points between 1997 and 2000, from 68 percent to 79 percent.[3]

Ten Tips for Enhanced Computer Security

There is no such thing as a 100 percent safe computer system. However, companies and institutions that want to limit risks and prosper in the age of electronic communication and commerce would do well to dedicate appropriate financial, human, and technological resources to information security.

Developing a computer security policy that adheres to the following basic security measures will help get your organization's program off to a good start.[4]

1. Install Firewalls with Secure Passwords

The most common way to protect your computer network is to install firewall software to filter out unwanted intruders. If you install a firewall properly and assign it a secure password, the software should do a good job of keeping your electronic assets safe. But that is not always the case.

Why do firewalls fail? Human error. Firewalls are only as effective as the people who install and maintain them. Failure to maintain a corporate firewall properly can leave your organization open to a potentially disastrous security breach. If you install a protective firewall, but then neglect to establish a proper firewall security policy, it will fail. Similarly, if you install a firewall that is not adequate for your specific application or experience level, it will fail.

Don't forget to upgrade your firewall to keep intruders out. More knowledgeable about computer vulnerabilities than most business executives, malicious hackers know that many organizations never bother to upgrade their firewalls to the current version or revision.

2. Make Sure Your Perimeter Firewalls and Routers Are Installed and Maintained Correctly

Clearly, the success of external computer security is tied closely to human performance. Your security software tools are only as effective as your ability to correctly install, accurately maintain, and effectively operate them.

A common area of vulnerability is the improper configuration of firewalls, routers, and other network components critical to computer security. Configuration errors can occur when components are installed in haste or are positioned incorrectly by individuals who do not know how to configure components for security purposes.

At large companies with experienced in-house security teams who regularly install and maintain computer security applications, configuration problems are the biggest concern. Smaller operations that have Internet exposures but lack internal security capabilities should tap the expertise of their network administrators or third-party security consultants to ensure they are protected by the right applications, and that their computer network has a secure design.

3. Install Encryption Coding to Safeguard the Transmission of Electronic Data

The American Society for Industrial Security cites computer penetration as one of the top three methods of stealing proprietary information.[5] Protect your confidential company information by drafting an e-policy that restricts or outlaws the nonencrypted electronic transmission and/or storage of trade secrets and other proprietary information. That's the human solution. The technical answer: Use encryption algorithms to scramble e-mail messages and files and keep private information out of intruders' hands.

4. Assign Network Administrators a Security Role

Your network administrator no doubt knows your computer system inside and out. As such, network administrators can play a valuable role by identifying and solving security problems. Nonetheless, many employers never call upon their own network administrators to get involved in security.

A busy network administrator or network administration team, particularly one employed by a smaller company, may not have time to address vast security needs. Network administrators typically are responsible for adding new segments to the network, bringing up new servers, installing system software, maintaining the system, controlling viruses, learning new applications, and helping customers. With all that activity on their schedules, most are left with little or no time to address security concerns.

Organizations eager to manage their electronic risks internally would do well to assign network administrators a security role. If cost is an issue, rest assured that the cost to restore your computer system and/or fund litigation should your breached system be used to access a business partner's computer network would far exceed the cost of beefing up your network administrator team.

5. Hire an Outside Security Consultant

Don't have a full-time security officer or security team in place? Want to check your internal security team's effectiveness? Aren't interested in assigning your network administrator a security role? Then consider hiring a third-party expert to perform security functions on a less permanent, less costly basis.

Familiar with the most common configuration errors and computer security gaps, a consultant can be retained to conduct a thorough assessment of your network, identify vulnerabilities, and recommend fixes. Once your organization's security problems are identified, either your network administrator or your paid consultant can get to work putting the expert's recommended solutions into place.

6. Conduct Periodic Security Audits

Eager to keep pace with competitors, most organizations regularly adjust their networks and upgrade their software. With those improvements, however, come new vulnerabilities.

Don't be lulled into believing that a one-time computer security assessment will make your organization safe and keep it safe forever. Conduct periodic computer system security audits to assess your current security situation and correct any problems that may have developed since your last audit.

7. Don't Ignore Small Company Security Needs

Any organization with e-mail and an Internet presence has security risks. A company that operates an information-only Web site may not face risks as great as a transactional site, but the exposures and potential costs are just as real. A smaller organization's Web site, for example, may be linked to the back office computer system, where payroll and other private information reside. The receipt of virus-infected e-mail messages or attachments could crash the system in no time, laying waste to the company's critical data.

Smaller companies would do well to combine security basics—a single firewall and antivirus software—with comprehensive e-mail and Internet policies to keep human intruders at bay and exterminate electronic bugs.

8. Limit Access to Your Computer Room

Taking steps as basic as requiring employees to log onto the system and limiting physical access to the computer room can play a substantial role in enhancing security and reducing risks. If intruders are going to crack your system, at least make them work for it.

9. Educate Employees about the Dangers of Social Engineering

As a rule, hackers will do extensive research before penetrating a site. Intelligence gathering includes learning all they can about the target and its site, sweeping a network to determine exposures, and visiting one of the estimated 1900 hacker Web sites that offer digital tools to facilitate snooping, crashing, and hijacking control of computers.[6]

Depending on the target organization's location and the intruder's interest, a hacker may do a little social engineering as well. Social engineering is the process through which outsiders take advantage of an employee's naïveté or a company's carelessness to get their hands on passwords or other information that will help them gain access to your network.

For example, if you print e-mail addresses on your business cards (and who doesn't?), you are opening yourself up to attack. Armed with nothing more than an e-mail address, a hacker can start to gather information about your computer network, determine what type of hardware and software are on your system, and deploy standard, proven-effective attacks against your applications in an attempt to gain access.

Social engineering often is decidedly low-tech. Let's say, for example, that your organization is in the process of relocating to a new office building. Aware that your new offices are still under construction, a hacker easily could don a hard hat and tool belt, stroll past your receptionist, and enter your server room. If your server room resembles many others, the hacker likely would find your administrative passwords taped to a wall. Congratulations. You have just handed the keys to your network to a stranger whose intentions are questionable at best.

Pay equal attention to the exterior of your building. A trash container can be a treasure-trove for hackers looking for discarded customer lists, employee identification cards, and network information. Prevent what hackers refer to as "dumpster diving" by investing in a shredder and making its use a mandatory part of your e-security program.

10. Teach Employees about Hackers

What's one of the most effective ways to reduce the likelihood of social engineering? Training. People are less likely to be vulnerable to the manipulations of trouble-making intruders if they understand something about hackers and their motivations.

Many hackers are technically astute people who mean no harm but simply enjoy the challenge of breaking into a system. Young people who crack into big-name companies just to grab data and show off to their hacker friends fall into this category. Other, more unscrupulous hackers seek financial gain by stealing credit card numbers or personal financial information.

Corporations have been known to employ hackers to steal trade secrets from competitors. Law firms have hired hackers to look for evidence to support legal claims. The media have been known to hack as part of the research process. Advertisers, looking for a competitive edge, have hacked onto sites in search of demographic data and information about shopping habits.

Even governments are getting into the act. Some foreign governments have made it clear that they would rather pay a hacker a few million dollars to steal information from U.S. corporations than devote hundreds of millions of dollars and years of effort to research and development.

Form a Security Posse

Explain to your employees that hackers are not always strangers. A hacker can just as easily be the disgruntled employee sitting in the next cubicle as an unknown cybervillain lurking in the shadows. In fact, law enforcement officials estimate that up to 60 percent of system break-ins are the work of employees.[7]

Internal saboteurs can do tremendous damage to your computer system and your organization's business operations. Take the case of the disgruntled computer programmer who was charged with zapping Omega Engineering Corp.'s computer system, causing losses of $10 million to this manufacturer of high-tech measurement and control devices that are used by the U.S. Navy and NASA.[8] On a smaller, but no less disturbing scale, a computer technician hired by Forbes, Inc. on a temporary basis was charged with breaking into the publisher's system and causing a computer crash that cost the company more than $100,000.[9]

Similarly, your employees may hack your system to exact some form of revenge, embezzle funds, sabotage operations, cause the company embarrassment, undermine a career, or subvert a deal. An employee who conducts an unauthorized search of co-workers' salaries and benefits, either to force a raise from management or cause embarrassment to an individual or the organization, is guilty of hacking. A more extreme example would be a technically astute employee who, bent on revenge for what the employee perceived to be unfair treatment by management, changed everyone's password. In the process, the employee/hacker would deny system access across the board and trigger an unexpected and potentially devastating interruption of business.

Armed with a basic understanding of who hackers are and how they operate, your employees can play an informal security role. Encourage employees to report suspected security breaches, hacker activity, and just plain odd behavior to the organization's CIO. Keep employees alert to e-risks by holding periodic security training sessions. And reward employees who succeed in helping you keep malicious hackers out of the system.

Chapter 5 Recap and E-Action Plan: Enhancing Computer Security to Reduce Malicious Attacks and Financial Loss

1. Security technology does not equal a security program. Enhance your organization's computer security by implementing a comprehensive information security program, complete with trained security professionals, a comprehensive security policy, a security awareness program for employees, and a security structure that addresses the needs and challenges of your industry and computing environment.

2. Conduct periodic security audits and upgrade security policies, procedures, tools, and software as necessary.

3. Adhere faithfully to The E-Policy Handbook's 10 Tips for Enhanced Computer Security.

Using Cyberinsurance Policies to Help Manage E-Risks

With all the news about hackers infiltrating Internet sites and bringing online businesses to a halt, you might think your organization is defenseless against attacks from outside hackers and internal saboteurs. Not so. According to the e-insurance experts at Assurex International, both traditional insurance products and newly introduced cyberinsurance policies can protect any organization with an e-mail or Internet system from the risks associated with doing business online.[1]

From high-flying dot-com companies to traditional businesses with a Web presence, any organization that operates a corporate e-mail system or uses the Internet to dispense information or sell services or products faces myriad risks. Inappropriate or off-color e-mail messages can lead to employee lawsuits. Denial of service attacks and computer viruses can interrupt business, draining revenues and destroying corporate credibility. Failure to deliver products or services as advertised on the Internet can trigger lawsuits. The improper downloading or posting of copyrighted or trademarked material can lead to litigation. The list of e-risks is seemingly endless. Fortunately, cyberinsurance products offer comprehensive protections that can help reduce the likelihood of costly, protracted lawsuits.

The experts at Assurex International, the world's largest privately held commercial insurance brokerage group, note that some of the best protections for clicks-and-mortar companies come from insurance products that have long served bricks-and-mortar businesses. In fact, the insurance policies many organizations need to mitigate their e-risks may be standard coverages applied to the Internet, rather than specialized cyberinsurance products.

What's the best advice for organizations that want to reduce their e-liabilities? Assurex recommends you consult with an insurance broker experienced with cyber-risks and e-insurance products. Then, working with your risk management team, establish a comprehensive cyberinsurance program to protect your organization from the e-risks specific to your company.

Following are insurance products that companies engaged in electronic communication or e-commerce may want to consider. These products are listed to give employers an idea of the type of insurance protections available. They should not be purchased without consulting an experienced e-insurance broker.

Employment Practices Liability Insurance Helps Limit E-Mail Risks

Almost all organizations have e-mail systems. Even with a written policy, the potential for disaster from employee misuse and abuse of e-mail is significant. If just one employee sends an off-color joke, racist remark, sexist comment, or pornographic photo via your e-mail system, you could find yourself in a legal battle with other employees who felt harassed or offended by the inappropriate message. That's where employment practices liability insurance (EPLI) comes into play.

EPLI, which protects employers from workers' claims of discrimination or wrongful termination based on race, sex, age, or disability, is a must for any organization that grants employees access to e-mail. EPLI also can protect your organization from third-party liability claims filed by customers and other outsiders who are offended by messages carried by your organization's e-mail system or inadvertently posted on your Web site.

Savvy employers seeking to limit the risks of discrimination and harassment lawsuits would do well to combine a zero-tolerance attitude with an effectively written, clearly communicated e-mail policy and an employment practices liability insurance policy.

Crisis Communications Coverage Helps You Recover from E-Disaster

As detailed in Chapters 4 and 5, you can protect your organization from a certain amount of internal misuse and external abuse by establishing a written e-risk management policy and enforcing computer security procedures. Unfortunately, though, even with the best software tools and most comprehensive written policies in place, electronic disasters can strike.

For example, if a hacker launched a denial of service attack against your system, you might lose face along with revenues if the media reported on your inability to get back online in a timely fashion. Were an executive to be arrested for using the company's Internet system to solicit sex from minors, your company's good name could be dragged through the mud along with the offending employee's reputation. Were a staff member to use the company's e-mail system to organize a white supremacist group, you could find yourself in the position of fighting an expensive lawsuit while attempting to quiet a public uproar.

A small business or a private company might be able to weather an e-crisis quietly, but a company that is publicly traded or boasts a household name most likely would find itself trapped in the glare of the media spotlight for the duration of the crisis.

To offset the costs associated with e-crises, your organization may want to purchase a crisis communications insurance policy. Crisis communications insurance is designed to fund post-crisis damage control, enabling you to hire the best PR consultants to cast your company's story in the most favorable light. Crisis communications insurance is expensive, and it is not for everyone. It may, however, make sense for high-profile dot-coms and larger organizations whose post-crisis PR and legal fees could stretch into six or seven figures.

Smaller companies that lack funds to invest in crisis communications insurance should nonetheless address crisis communications as part of their overall e-mail and Internet policies. See Chapter 19 for specific guidelines on developing a written crisis communications plan for your organization, regardless of industry or size.

Ward Off Bugs with Computer Virus Transmission Coverage

While there is no way to ensure that bugs never get into your system, you can take steps to reduce the likelihood of viruses.

Reduce the risk of computer viruses by discussing e-mail attachments in your written e-mail policy. E-mail attachments are the most common means of spreading viruses. At a minimum, inform employees they are not permitted to open attachments sent by unknown parties. Some organizations go even further, prohibiting employees from opening any e-mail attachment, regardless of the sender. While a total prohibition may keep viruses out of your computer system, it does so at the expense of a valuable e-mail benefit: the ability to transmit documents quickly and inexpensively.

You can gain greater protection against bugs by establishing a written software usage policy. Employees who download software from the Internet or bring personal software into the office from home may unwittingly carry viruses into the workplace. A written software usage policy that prohibits downloading and copying unlicensed software will reduce the likelihood of electronic bugs.

As detailed in Chapter 5, you should install antivirus software as part of your organization's basic computer security program.

Unfortunately, while virus software and written policies will go a long way toward helping you reduce the risk of viruses, no preventive measure is totally effective. After all, what good are written guidelines if you employ scofflaws who ignore your policies and download virus-laden software that crashes your system and erases your files? What protections can antivirus software offer against new viruses that are resistant to existing technology?

New cyberinsurance products can help. Where preventive measures sometimes fail, computer virus transmission insurance succeeds. Regardless of how a bug enters your system, computer virus transmission insurance will help cover the cost to restore your system to good health.

Insure against Copyright and Trademark Infringement with Media Liability Coverage

If your company is using the Internet as a sales and marketing tool, you are exposing yourself to significant intellectual property risks, most notably copyright and trademark infringement. To limit risks, be sure to address copyright law and copyright infringement issues within your e-mail, Internet, and software usage policies. Make sure employees—particularly those responsible for writing the company's Web site copy, e-mail newsletter, e-zine, and other online publications—know that it is illegal to download, copy, or use copyrighted or trademarked material without permission of the work's author.

For added protection, implement copy clearance procedures with your organization's intellectual property lawyer to ensure that the material you post on your Web site does not violate a copyright or trademark and is not libelous.

You can support those efforts by purchasing a media liability insurance policy to protect your organization against financial losses you would suffer if, in spite of your best efforts, you were sued for intellectual property infringement.

Patent Infringement Coverage Insures against Multimillion-Dollar Claims

Patent infringement lawsuits can mean years of big-bucks litigation. According to the cyberinsurance experts at Assurex, patent infringement claims are the most expensive liability claims, with defense costs averaging $1 million and judgments sometimes running as high as hundreds of millions of dollars.

Fortunately, patent infringement insurance is available to help employers manage this risk. Patent infringement insurance covers legal defense costs for companies that are accused of stealing other organizations' technologies. Policies also are available to fund litigation for smaller dot-com and e-commerce companies embroiled in patent infringement issues with corporate giants.

Given the high cost of patent claims, insurance coverage would seem to be the ideal solution for any organization that holds a patent, has filed for a patent, or has developed new technology for the Internet. However, patent infringement insurance coverage is expensive, with premiums ranging from $20,000 to $200,000 or more a year.

The best advice: Review your risks with a cyberinsurance broker who knows your company, understands your industry, and is experienced with patent infringement risks and polices. An experienced e-insurance broker can help determine if your risks warrant an investment in patent infringement insurance.

Fight Cyberterrorism with Extortion and Reward Coverage

Imagine receiving notice that a hacker is planning to crash your server, shut down operations, and violate the privacy of your employees and customers unless a multimillion-dollar ransom is paid. That's a pretty scary scenario, particularly for organizations that maintain employees' and clients' confidential files, for example, sensitive medical records.

Protect your organization from cyberterrorists by developing and enforcing a written e-risk management policy, implementing computer security procedures, and educating employees about the dangers of hackers and the risks of social engineering (see Chapter 5). Hope for the best but prepare for the worst by putting an extortion and reward insurance policy in place to respond to Internet extortion demands and pay rewards to help capture saboteurs.

Cover Third-Party Losses with Unauthorized Access/Unauthorized Use Coverage

Not all intruders are willing to take time to issue an extortion demand or sit around waiting for a ransom to be paid. Some cyberthieves prefer to take the money and run. If, in spite of your computer security efforts, a hacker gains access to your Web site and steals data or funds, an unauthorized access/unauthorized use insurance policy would cover you for failure to protect against third-party access to data and financial transactions.

Specialized Network Security Coverage Helps Guard Confidential Data

The explosion of Internet transactions has generated specific risks related to the handling of private information. Let's say your company operates an online staffing program in which your clients record their employees' salaries and benefits. If your security were breached and your clients' employees subsequently learned salary package details, you could be sued for failure to protect that confidential information. A specialized network security insurance policy would respond to that liability or any other breach of network security and resulting loss.

Computer Software and Services E&O Coverage Insures against Advice, Service, or Product Failure

Is your company using the Internet to dispense professional advice or sell services or products? If so, consider the protection offered by computer software and services errors and omissions (E&O) insurance. Those most in need of this kind of coverage are firms whose professional advice, services, or products, if flawed, could cause financial loss to a client.

For example, let's say a software developer creates an accounting package that is designed to absorb and retain all the customer's existing data. When the customer downloads the software, however, rather than absorbing and retaining data, it erases everything. The customer could opt to sue the software manufacturer under a computer software and services E&O claim for selling a flawed product that caused the loss. With computer software and services E&O insurance, the manufacturer likely would be covered.

Product Liability Insurance Covers Product Failures

If your company is using the Net to sell products, cover your risks by purchasing a product liability insurance policy. Product liability coverage, typically included in most general liability policies, will mitigate your exposure should the products you sell online cause bodily injury or property damage to a third party.

Directors' and Officers' Coverage Protects Business and Personal Assets

When lawsuits alleging wrongful acts occur, such as mismanagement, fiscal irresponsibility, or violations of security laws, corporations, directors, and officers may be at risk. For publicly traded dot-com companies, which are exposed to allegations of SEC violations, directors' and officers' (D&O) coverage is a must. Assurex International recommends public and private dot-coms alike consider D&O coverage to protect corporate assets as well as the personal assets of directors and officers.

Business Interruption Coverage Can Help Keep You Up and Running

If your computer system goes down and prevents you from conducting business, you likely will suffer a loss of revenue, credibility, productivity, and customers. Conventional business interruption insurance can help control your losses.

You can couple your business interruption insurance policy with a written crisis communications plan (Chapter 19) to ensure that you survive your period of business interruption intact, with minimal public relations, customer relations, or investor relations damage.

Guard against E-Theft with Crime Loss Insurance

Do you operate an online bank or payroll company? Is your firm a repository for financial assets? If so, crime loss insurance is available to protect your organization from liability related to the electronic theft of funds.

Be sure to back up your crime loss policy with a written e-risk management policy, computer security procedures, and employee education. Exert every effort to keep electronic thieves out and you may never need to make a claim against your crime loss policy.

Protect Your Computer Assets with Electronic Data Processing (EDP) Coverage

Depending on the size of your company and the industry in which you operate, you may have spent five, six, or even seven figures on computer hardware and software. With network additions and software upgrades, your investment just keeps growing. An EDP insurance policy can help you protect your computer assets.

EDP policies offer broader coverage for computer equipment damage than is normally found in a general business property policy. EDP policies cover hardware and software replacement costs, as well as extra expenses, such as the cost to hire technical experts and others to work overtime to recapture data following a crash. Some policies also offer and/or can be extended to cover loss of data caused by a computer virus.

Chapter 6 Recap and E-Action Plan: Insuring against Online Risks

1. Form an e-risk management partnership with your computer security consultant and insurance broker. Conduct a top-to-bottom assessment of your organization's e-risks and your ability to manage risks with employee training and the most effective software tools.

2. Consult with an insurance broker experienced with cyberrisks and e-insurance policies. Establish a comprehensive cyberinsurance program to help limit liabilities and control e-risks specific to your company and industry. Work with your broker

to keep pace with new cyberinsurance products as they are developed.

3. Keep your e-insurance broker in the loop regarding computer system enhancements and changes. If you make the transition from dispensing information to selling products online, let your insurance broker know. If you institute sweeping new computer security measures, alert your broker. The changes you make can have an impact on risks and premiums.

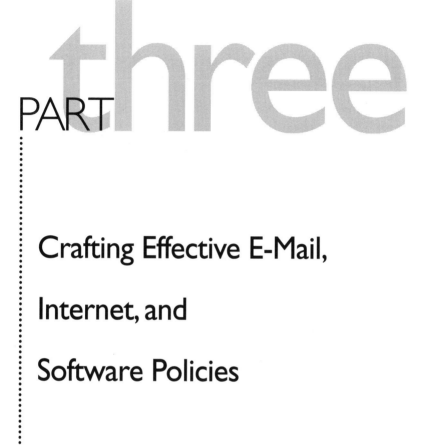

PART **three**

Crafting Effective E-Mail,

Internet, and

Software Policies

The Basics of E-Policy Development

By allowing employees access to e-mail and the Internet, employers have created one more avenue down which they can be dragged into litigation. And since the laws and regulations governing cyberspace are not developing as quickly as the technology, it is incumbent upon employers to take action to protect themselves.

One of the best protections available to employers is a comprehensive e-policy that clearly defines what is and is not acceptable use of the organization's computer assets. Regardless of whether you employ a staff of two part-timers or 2000 full-time professionals, there is no reason not to implement e-mail, Internet, and software usage policies. There are, however, plenty of compelling reasons to do so.

If you think a brief, informal policy along the lines of, "The company's computer system is reserved for business use only," will protect you, think again. Regardless of the industry in which you operate or the number of people you employ, it is important to give employees consistently enforced rules to work by.

While brief is bad, you also want to avoid policies that are excessively long or intimidating. As detailed in Chapter 16, presentation plays an important role in e-policy success. If your written policy is long on words and short on white space, your employees may never take time to read it from beginning to end.

The best advice: Keep policies simple. Keep policies straightforward. Make policies accessible.

General Guidelines for Effective E-Mail, Internet, and Software Usage Policies

1. Effective e-policies should be written documents. Form an e-policy team of experts to draft your documents for senior management's review and approval.

2. Take your approved policies to an experienced employment lawyer or cyberlaw expert. Have the policies reviewed for completeness, accuracy, and adherence to federal and state laws and regulations. While you're at it, this would be a good time to have all your human resources policies reviewed.

3. Following the legal review and management's approval of any required changes, incorporate your e-mail, Internet, and software usage policies into your organization's printed employee handbook. Make it easy for employees to access and review your e-policies as needs arise.

4. Your written e-policies should spell out clearly what is, and is not, allowed to be communicated via your organization's e-mail and Internet systems. They also should address the legal and ethical use of software.

5. Use your e-policies to inform employees of their electronic rights and responsibilities. Address privacy. Make sure employees know exactly what they can expect in terms of monitoring. Review the e-risks faced by your company. Stress the repercussions employees will face should they violate the organization's written e-policies.

6. Make the development and implementation of your e-policies a companywide initiative. Review your e-policies with all employees, including full-time, part-time, and temporary staff, as well as independent contractors and freelancers who work on behalf of your organization. Educate managers and supervisors about the importance of consistently enforcing the organization's e-policies. Make sure every new hire receives e-policy orientation,

along with the organization's other get-acquainted literature and training.

7. Let your employees know you mean business. Designed primarily to protect your organization from employee misuse and hacker abuse of your computer assets, thoughtfully written, thoroughly communicated e-policies also will protect your employees from themselves. Employees who know and understand your organization's e-policies and the penalties violators will face for noncompliance are less likely to get themselves and the organization into e-trouble by sending offensive e-mail messages, surfing inappropriate Internet sites, breaching established computer security procedures, or copying software illegally.

8. Remember that writing comprehensive e-mail, Internet, and software policies is only half the battle. To win the war against e-risks, you must back up policy development with ongoing training. Hold a seminar or series of seminars to introduce employees to your e-policies, being careful to explain why you have implemented the policies, what you expect from each employee, and how policy violators will be dealt with.

   Following initial training, create ways to reinforce the organization's goal of 100 percent policy compliance. Hold brief e-consciousness-raising sessions to update employees about new risks, regulations, and related issues. Send out periodic reminders via e-mail. Stuff e-policy statements in employees' paycheck envelopes.

9. Control risks by controlling content. Incorporate an electronic writing policy into your comprehensive e-policy. Your e-writing policy will ensure that employees are maximizing the effectiveness of their electronic communication. (See Part 4.)

10. Establish netiquette policies for e-mail senders and receivers. Address the special electronic etiquette concerns of managers and employees. (See Chapter 9.)

11. Use your comprehensive e-policy to set language guidelines for employees. Outlaw the use of sexist language and turnoff words

that could offend or repel readers. Make it clear that obscene, harassing, or otherwise offensive language will not be tolerated. Without coming across as overly harsh or somber, prohibit the telling of jokes via e-mail. Unless you employ professional humorists, jokes can lead to misunderstanding, hurt feelings, and lawsuits. Also use your cyberlanguage policy to address smileys and emoticons, abbreviations, technical language, jargon, and other language issues of concern to you and your employees. (See Chapter 15.)

12. Hope for the best but prepare for the worst. By taking steps to manage risks, establish security procedures, and address employee e-mail, Internet, and software usage, you will be better able to avert cybercrises before they happen.

   Don't rely on chance. All it takes is one hacker attack, a single incident of software piracy, or one carelessly worded e-mail message for you to find yourself facing intense media and public scrutiny. Be prepared. Incorporate an e-crisis communications plan into your overall e-policy. (See Chapter 19.)

13. Stay current. The worlds of e-commerce and e-communication are changing rapidly. Cyberlaws and government regulations are evolving, as are cyberinsurance and e-security products. Damaging and potentially deadly computer viruses are infecting systems with increasing frequency. New e-products, including antihacking and monitoring software, are being introduced to the marketplace regularly.

   The e-mail and Internet policies you develop this year may not serve your needs twelve months from now. Meet regularly with your cyberlawyer to review your e-policies and make necessary revisions.

14. Don't forget to follow up with employee training to cover any new aspects of your e-policies. Maintain documentation to prove when employees received exactly which version of what policy. As new versions of each policy are adopted, have employees review and sign them.

It's Time to Get to Work on E-Policy Development

Chapters 8 through 11 are designed to guide your organization through the development of effective e-mail, Internet, and software usage policies. See Appendixes A and C for sample policies.

Chapter 7 Recap and E-Action Plan: An E-Policy Development Primer

1. Protect your company from your employees and your employees from themselves by developing and implementing written e-mail, Internet, and software usage policies.

2. Consult with an experienced employment law or cyberlaw expert to ensure your policies' accuracy, thoroughness, and compliance with federal and state laws.

3. Make clear to employees what they can and cannot expect in terms of e-mail and Internet privacy and monitoring.

4. Make your e-policy program a top-to-bottom, companywide initiative. Develop ongoing training programs for all employees, from part-time interns to senior executives and owners.

5. Incorporate comprehensive writing, language, and netiquette guidelines as part of your overall e-policy.

6. Be prepared. Draft an e-crisis communications policy to limit risks should you be hit with a denial of service attack or other electronic disaster.

7. Consult with experts in the areas of cyberlaw, e-risk management, computer security, and cyberinsurance. Stay on top of legal issues, technology, and insurance products that could help you manage workplace risks.

E-Mail Policy Considerations
Think before You Send

E-mail may be the quickest and easiest way to communicate, but that does not necessarily make it the most appropriate way to conduct business. Advise employees to think before they write. Assess each situation individually to determine whether the message is best communicated via e-mail, or if the telephone or a face-to-face meeting might be better.[1]

Instruct Employees to Avoid E-Mail When ...

1. A message is extremely important or confidential and you cannot risk a breach of privacy. Never use e-mail to communicate proprietary corporate information. With millions of hidden readers and dastardly hackers lurking in cyberspace, e-mail simply is not secure.

2. You want to conduct negotiations or hold a give-and-take conversation. Whether you want to negotiate a price reduction with a supplier or persuade your supervisor to give you a pay raise, dialogues that call for back-and-forth discussion are best held on the phone or in person.

3. You need to conduct a lengthy interview with a long list of questions that call for detailed answers.

4. You want to deliver bad news or discuss an emotionally charged matter. Without the benefit of facial expressions, intonation, and body language, hurt feelings could ensue and flame wars could erupt if you deliver bad news electronically.

5. You seek an immediate response from someone who may not check e-mail regularly or has a tendency to procrastinate.

6. You want to involve a number of people in your discussion. This type of scenario calls for a teleconference, discussion-group software, or a bulletin board system rather than e-mail.

7. You run the risk of intimidating or turning off the reader with a written message.

8. You suspect your written message may be misunderstood or misconstrued.

Advise Employees to Use E-Mail When...

1. You want to deliver a message quickly and the speed with which you receive your reply does not matter. E-mail is a terrific way to send a quick message, but it is not necessarily the best route to a quick reply. Your reader is under no obligation to read or act upon your message in a timely fashion.

2. You want to communicate directly with the decision-maker, rather than fight your way past a gatekeeper. As long as you have the decision-maker's correct e-mail address, chances are your message will be read by your intended reader. Few people have assistants screen their e-mail.

   Bear in mind that senior executives are busy people. As such, they may be impatient with wordy or poorly constructed messages. Follow the organization's e-writing guidelines to ensure your e-mail messages are powerful, persuasive documents that motivate readers to act.

3. You want to avoid the cost of long-distance phone calls and faxes, local or overnight delivery services, or snail mail.

4. You need to communicate with a colleague or a customer in a different time zone or country and you don't want to get out of bed in the middle of the night to make a phone call. Thanks to e-mail, both the sender and the receiver can conduct business during normal working hours.

5. You want to deliver the same message to multiple readers. Whether it is a memo intended for six readers or an electronic newsletter with 6000 subscribers, e-mail makes it easy to deliver news quickly, easily, and inexpensively.

6. You need to maintain a written record of your electronic conversation. Before saving a message, however, review the company's document retention and deletion policy or ask your supervisor for authorization to store the e-mail.

7. You are on a tight deadline. If an assignment is due on the president's desk at 8:00 Monday morning, you can work all weekend, send the document Sunday night, and sleep soundly, knowing your material is sitting in the boss's mailbox awaiting review.

    Be careful not to wait until the last minute, however. Electronic delays and e-mail delivery problems sometimes occur. While the majority of messages are delivered without problems, there always is the possibility that your recipient's mail server will be down, keeping your message from getting through.

8. You want to communicate quickly and cost-effectively with co-workers. Why waste paper and time writing and distributing hard copies of memos when you can send internal e-mail messages with a click of your mouse? Just remember that the organization's netiquette policy (Chapter 9) and cyberlanguage guidelines (Chapter 15) apply to internal e-mail as well as external correspondence.

9. You need to stay in touch with the office and your customers when you are on the road. E-mail can be accessed from anywhere as long as you can log onto the Net. Electronic communication beats phone tag any time, particularly for weary travelers

caught between flight schedules, time zones, and competing priorities.

Attachment Guidelines for E-Mail Senders

The majority of e-mail messages are confined to one screen, and only a small portion of the screen at that. On occasion, however, there may be reason to send a much longer e-mail document. When the subject matter warrants it, go ahead and write a longer e-mail message. The reader may have to scroll through the screen to read it all. But that is not necessarily bad.

When it comes to message length, use common sense. If you think an e-mail message is going on too long, or you need to incorporate letterhead, charts, graphics, or lengthy copy into your message, then it is time to attach a separate document to your e-mail message. By using the attachment, you can add documents that have been created in separate files. Attachment software expands the capabilities of e-mail, allowing writers to send longer, more comprehensive documents, including word processing, spreadsheets, charts, and graphics.

Before attaching a document to your e-mail message, however, consider its appropriateness and the recipient's willingness to receive it. Employees should adhere to the following guidelines before sending an e-mail attachment.

1. Consider whether the recipient's e-mail system can accommodate your attachment. There is no point sending an attachment if your intended reader cannot or will not open it. Some organizations have strict policies that prohibit opening e-mail attachments. In these cases, information is best communicated within the confines of the e-mail message itself or delivered via snail mail, courier, or overnight delivery service.

   When in doubt about your reader's attachment policy, send a brief e-mail message or make a quick phone call prior to sending the first attachment. A little effort on the front end will save time and eliminate frustration down the road.

2. Attach first, write second. Have you ever received a message that introduces a nonexistent attachment? Avoid this common oversight by attaching your document first, then addressing and writing your e-mail message.

3. Use the attachment as intended. In your e-mail message, provide only a brief description of the attachment. Resist the temptation to go into detail. That is the attachment's job.

4. Generate reader interest in the attachment. Remember, most electronic readers are busy people who are trying to reduce, rather than expand, their workload. Don't risk your recipient ignoring or deleting your attachment unread. Use the brief description in your message to motivate the reader to open the attachment.

5. Be a courteous copier. The people to whom you send carbon copies and blind carbon copies will receive the attachment along with your e-mail message. That's a lot of information circulating through cyberspace. Copy only those persons who have a genuine need to read your e-mail message and its attachments.

6. Never send an attachment when a brief message will do. Before attaching a document to your e-mail, consider whether or not a brief message would accomplish your goal.

7. Compress extremely large files. Attaching extremely large files, such as databases, graphics, and spreadsheets, can be a problem. The time and resources needed to transmit and receive exceptionally large documents can irritate local network administrators and Internet service providers. As an alternative, consider using a compression program to reduce the size of large attachments. Before compressing, however, make sure your recipient has the capability to decompress the file.

Attachment Guidelines for E-Mail Receivers

E-mail attachments are the most common form of computer virus transportation. If you open an infected word-processing document, spreadsheet, or other attached document, there is a good chance you will catch a bug that could move swiftly through the entire organization, infecting one computer after another.

The best medicine is preventive. Virus protection software is a good first line of defense. But not even antivirus software can protect against all the new strains of virus that are in development, including those that are resistant to bug detectors.

The rules for employees are simple: (1) Never open an attachment unless you know the sender; and (2) Do not open an attachment if the message that accompanies it seems odd in any way. Even if you recognize the sender, don't take a chance. Delete the questionable message; then call the sender to express your concern. Be polite. After all, the message could turn out to be legitimate, only introduced by an odd subject line. If the message turns out to be bogus, the sender will thank you for the virus alert. If it is legitimate, ask the sender to transmit it again.

Forwarding E-Mail

While it is easy to forward a received message to one more reader or group of readers, employers may want to prohibit employees from doing so without permission from the original sender. A confidential e-mail message intended for a single reader could have a negative impact on the original sender if forwarded to additional, unintended readers.

Listserv Guidelines

Listservs are subscription-only e-mail lists that allow large numbers of participants to share information and discuss issues. An employee who belongs to a professional association, for example, may sign up for that association's listserv.

While providing a quick and convenient way to share information and hold electronic discussions, listservs can create problems for the recipient and the recipient's employer. A listserv may have dozens, hundreds, possibly thousands of subscribers. Every message and reply that is sent via the listserv is forwarded to every member. As a result, an employee who belongs to just one listserv could receive many messages on any given day. Should that employee join several listservs, the volume could increase to hundreds of e-mail messages a day. Multiply the time and resources wasted by a single listserv subscriber by the total number of employees in your organization and you could be facing a productivity nightmare.

Reduce the burden on your e-mail server and control your employees' online time by establishing guidelines to prohibit listserv participation. Consider outlawing listservs altogether, or restricting subscriptions to authorized, business-related listservs.

Writing Guidelines

Just because e-mail gets there faster does not mean you should spend less time sweating the mechanical details. All business correspondence, whether electronic or traditional, projects an image of the individual writer and the organization as a whole.

An e-mail document full of errors will tax the reader's patience and lessen the writer's credibility. In the battle for the reader's on-screen attention, carefully written e-mail that is free of mechanical errors is sure to come out the winner.

Supplement your e-mail policy with an electronic writing policy (see Part 4). Use your e-writing policy to provide employees with mechanical and stylistic guidelines, as well as cyberlanguage and netiquette rules.

To maximize the effectiveness of your employees' electronic writing, you may want to retain the services of a professional writing coach to review your e-writing policy with employees and conduct a series of business writing refresher courses for staff, managers, and executives.

Chapter 8 Recap and E-Action Plan: Establishing Guidelines for Appropriate E-Mail Use

1. Remind employees that e-mail, while the quickest means of business communication, is not always the most appropriate or effec-

tive way to deliver a message. Advise employees to think about their message, audience, and goal before they write. Some situations warrant a telephone call or a face-to-face meeting rather than an e-mail message.

2. One of the easiest ways to catch a computer virus is by opening an e-mail attachment. As part of your organization's e-mail policy, establish clear guidelines for sending and receiving attachments.

3. Needless electronic correspondence wastes your employees' time while clogging up your computer system. Establish guidelines for message forwarding and listserv participation.

4. Set electronic writing guidelines to help control content and improve the overall effectiveness of employee writing.

A Netiquette Primer for Employees and Managers

The power of e-mail is considerable. With e-mail, you can send a message around the globe as quickly and conveniently as you can communicate with an office mate. You can distribute lengthy documents across time zones and continents with just a click of your mouse. And you can respond to a client's inquiry or a supervisor's request in a matter of seconds.

With all that power, however, comes responsibility. Every e-mail message sent by an employee reflects upon your organization's credibility, not to mention the professionalism of the writer. Electronic documents that are poorly constructed and riddled with mechanical errors can turn off customers and sink careers. E-mail messages sent inadvertently to the wrong recipient can compromise confidences, create hard feelings, and cause embarrassment. Electronic correspondence that is menacing, harassing, pornographic, or otherwise inappropriate can trigger litigation.

An effective e-policy should incorporate a discussion of the rules of netiquette, or e-mail etiquette. By addressing and enforcing the rules of netiquette, employers can help reduce the likelihood of employees writing and sending the types of inappropriate messages that can offend readers and lead to workplace lawsuits.

Mind Your Electronic Manners

Use your e-mail policy to provide employees with basic guidelines for acceptable and effective electronic correspondence. By its nature, e-mail is a "cold" medium. Messages written and conversations held on-screen lack the warmth of face-to-face discussions and telephone calls, which benefit, respectively, from body language and intonation.

Couple its coldness with the tendency of many writers to type messages quickly, and sometimes thoughtlessly, and it is easy to see how e-mail can result in hurt feelings and misunderstandings.

Adherence to the basic rules of netiquette can alleviate problems and help cast your employees and your organization in a favorable light.

Establishing Netiquette Guidelines for Employees

Here are some guidelines you can use to create a netiquette policy for your employees.[1]

Beware Hidden Readers

If confidentiality is an issue, don't use e-mail. It's not secure. You may intend to send an e-mail to only one person, but an inaccurate keystroke or the recipient's decision to forward your message could land your e-mail on dozens, hundreds, or thousands of unintended readers' screens. Never use e-mail to communicate trade secrets, proprietary information, or any news that could damage the organization or its employees were the message to be read by an unintended reader.

Write as Though Mom Were Reading

Regardless of the intended reader, write your message as if your boss, the media, or Mom were looking over your shoulder. People treat e-mail too casually, sending electronic messages they would never record on paper. Don't write anything you would not feel comfortable saying in an elevator crowded with colleagues, customers, and competitors.

Remain Gender Neutral

You never know where your e-mail will land, so avoid sexist language that could offend or rankle others. Your intended reader may be a male, but the ultimate decision-maker could be the female executive (the hidden reader) who receives a forwarded copy of your original message. Sending a message full of masculine pronouns (he, his, him, etc.) could lose you an account for good. (See Chapter 15 for more on gender-neutral language.)

Keep the Organization's Harassment and Discrimination Policies in Mind

Sexual harassment and racial discrimination lawsuits have resulted from employees sending improper internal and external e-mail messages. All electronic communication should adhere to the rules set forth in the organization's harassment and discrimination policies.

Don't Use E-Mail to Let Off Steam

Upset or angry? Compose yourself before composing your message. Once you hit "send," your e-mail is on its way through cyberspace and probably can't be retrieved. Don't take the chance of sending a poorly worded message that could worsen an already difficult situation. If communication is urgently needed, ask a trusted colleague to read your document before you send it. If you have the luxury of time, give yourself a day or two to calm down before sending a potentially damaging message.

Control the Urge to Flame

More biting than a thoughtlessly worded message, an e-mail flame is a document that is hostile, blunt, rude, insensitive, or obscene. Flames are unique to e-mail, as the slow pace of snail mail does not accommodate immediate, heated reactions. Flames, and the obscene and abusive language that feed them, have no place in a business environment (or a personal one, for that matter).

Respect Readers' Time

An electronic mailbox that is stuffed with recipes, jokes, health warnings, advertisements, and requests for charitable donations can be a time-consuming annoyance. Do not use the company computer system to send or forward spam or electronic junk mail. Need convincing? In some states, spamming is against the law. A violation can get you a fine or possibly jail time.

Never Reply to Spam

If you are on the receiving end of a spam mailing, do not reply to the "unsubscribe" option. Often, your reply accomplishes just the opposite. Your reply confirms your e-mail address and may encourage the sender to forward your address to other spammers. Replying to spam also can be a waste of time, as senders sometimes use one-time-only addresses to blast their spam into cyberspace. Your irate reply could land in a black hole. So why bother?

Do Not Mail to the World

Send e-mail messages only to readers with a legitimate need for your information. Mail to your group list only when it is appropriate for everyone on the list to receive the message. Do not reply to a message unless you have something to contribute.

Copy with Care

Sending a carbon copy (Cc) or blind carbon copy (Bcc) to a recipient who doesn't need to read your message wastes everyone's time. As a rule, address your message to the person you want to motivate to act and send carbon copies strictly as a courtesy. Carbon copy recipients are not required to reply to messages. So don't get upset when a response is not forthcoming.

Don't Oversell Your Message

Just because you have the ability to mark messages "urgent" doesn't mean you should. Reserve the urgent classification for messages that demand immediate action. Otherwise, you may develop a reputation as a writer who values your own time above your reader's.

Ask Permission to Forward Material

Do you subscribe to an e-zine or electronic newsletter that may be of interest to an associate or customer? Don't hit "forward" without asking permission from the individual who originally sent the material as well as your intended recipient.

Inquire about Attachments

Some organizations prohibit the opening of e-mail attachments. Before sending an attachment, ask if the reader would prefer to receive the information as an attachment or in the field as part of the message itself.

Incorporate a Salutation and Signature

A salutation and signature will establish your role in the document's history, no matter how often it's forwarded. As an added benefit, your signature signals the end, sparing your reader the aggravation of scrolling the screen for more copy.

Beware the Exclamation Point!!!

Some writers try to enliven their e-mail and generate reader interest by slapping an exclamation point onto the end of nearly every sentence. Don't fall into this trap. Pump up your writing with descriptive language and well-crafted sentences.

Resist the Urge to Capitalize

Eager for reader attention, many e-mail writers use all capital letters. That's a bad idea on two counts. For one thing, the eye is accustomed to reading a mix of capital and lowercase letters. Writing uppercase-only messages will slow the reader down and may impede understanding and acceptance of your message.

Another concern is that readers sometimes interpret messages written in capital letters as a form of shouting. If you write entirely in the uppercase, you run the risk of losing recipients before they ever start reading. Do yourself and your readers a favor: Stick with standard sentence style.

Apply the Same Rule to Lowercase Letters

Some people think an e-mail message that's written entirely in lowercase letters conveys a breezy, informal tone. No. Business correspondence that is written entirely in the lowercase is likely to give the impression that you are lazy and unprofessional in your writing.

Keep an Eye on Spelling, Grammar, and Punctuation

Your readers will. You wouldn't walk into the president's office or a customer's showroom and start speaking gibberish. Why, then, would you send an e-mail message that is a written form of gibberish? Professionalism extends to all forms of communication: written, verbal, and electronic.

Think before Requesting a Receipt

Imagine writing a crucial e-mail message that must be read and acted upon. Short of receiving an electronic response, how can you be certain your message has been received and read?

The quickest, easiest route to peace of mind is to select the "receipt notification" option on your screen. When the reader opens your message, you will be notified automatically. Exercise this option with caution, however. Some readers will resent the implication that you do not trust them to open and read their e-mail. In a pressing situation, the better option might be to phone your recipient with a quick heads-up that the message is on its way and you would appreciate a timely response.

Keep Your Editorial Comments to Yourself

If you receive an e-mail message that is short on style but long on mechanical and grammatical errors, keep your editorial comments to yourself. Just as few speakers appreciate having their grammar corrected publicly by co-workers, few e-mail writers enjoy receiving unsolicited critiques of their electronic writing. Leave that job to management or the professional writing coach management hires to help employees polish their electronic and business writing skills.

Treat Others as You Would Have Them Treat You

If you receive someone else's e-mail by mistake, don't trash it. Hit "reply" to redirect it to the sender, along with a brief note about the mix-up.

Consider E-Mail's Limitations

E-mail may be the best way to deliver news fast, but it's not necessarily the best route to a quick reply. Your reader is under no obligation to check incoming messages regularly, if at all. And it is inappropriate to send a follow-up message demanding to know why a recipient has not responded to your message.

For an immediate response to a pressing issue, don't rely on e-mail. Instead, pick up the phone or schedule a face-to-face meeting.

Special Netiquette Considerations for Managers

Executives and managers should, of course, adhere to the basic rules of netiquette as outlined above. In addition, there are a handful of special netiquette considerations that apply solely to those who supervise employees. Consider the following guidelines when developing your netiquette policy for managers.

1. On a regular basis, managers should remind employees that the organization has the right to monitor employee e-mail and Internet use. Don't allow employees to develop an expectation of privacy when it comes to the organization's computer assets. Following the initial introduction of the organization's e-mail policy, managers should create opportunities to remind employees that Big Brother may be reading over their electronic shoulders at any given moment.

2. Managers should enforce the organization's e-mail policy consistently and equally. Do not allow managers, supervisors, or senior staff any special e-rights that other employees cannot enjoy equally.

If the organization's e-policy states that employees will be terminated for sending e-mail messages that violate sexual harassment guidelines, managers must follow through by firing all violators. The only way the organization's e-mail policy will succeed at reducing liability risks is if it is enforced consistently. No exceptions.

3. Managers should be realistic about the company's personal use policy. While e-mail is intended for business use, most organizations accept a limited amount of personal use. E-mail may be the only way for some employees to keep in touch with children and spouses during working hours. Working parents who are prohibited from communicating with family members via e-mail may decide to look for a more family-friendly employer.

4. Managers should never use e-mail to fire employees or deliver other bad news. Without the benefit of body language, facial expression, or intonation, e-mail is the worst way to deliver bad news to employees. Whether your objective is to terminate an employee or notify a department head of budgetary cutbacks, demonstrate respect for your employees by delivering bad news in person. A one-on-one meeting will give the employee the opportunity to ask questions and absorb shock. Should a wrongful termination lawsuit follow, personal notification will cast management in a better light than electronic notification would.

5. Managers should not use e-mail to discuss an employee's performance with other managers. Managers are not required to like every employee on a personal level, but they are obligated to treat each worker with professional courtesy. If a manager needs to discuss an employee's professional shortcomings with the human resources director or instruct a department head to terminate an employee who just isn't working out, this discussion should be held in person and behind closed doors.

E-mail is fraught with too many dangers for sensitive or confidential communication. Strike your group list key accidentally and you could send negative comments about an employee to everyone in the organization. Type in the address of the employee in question, rather than the human resources director, and the employee (and the employee's lawyer) would be alerted to management's negative feelings and comments.

Worst case scenario: If the employee in question were to file a workplace lawsuit, alleging a hostile work environment or wrongful termination, the manager's electronic discussion with the human resources director could come back to haunt the company. E-mail messages, like written performance reviews and other documents, can be subject to discovery and subpoena in litigation. In the event of trial, e-mail messages concerning this employee could be used as evidence against the organization.

Unless writers are willing to risk a breach of security and have their words read by unintended readers, they should not use e-mail. It simply is not secure.

6. Managers should not rely on e-mail to the exclusion of personal contact. To varying degrees, employees, customers, and suppliers all crave human interaction. While some people may be content to communicate electronically nearly 100 percent of the time, others may feel slighted or unappreciated unless you maintain ongoing personal contact. Even in the age of e-mail, relationship skills remain at the heart of long-term business success. Managers should supplement electronic communication with periodic staff, customer, and supplier meetings.

7. Managers should not use e-mail when there is any chance a message will be misunderstood. If a message is complex, technical, or otherwise in any danger of being misinterpreted, opt for a telephone call or a personal meeting instead of e-mail.

8. Managers should not rely solely on e-mail to communicate e-policies to employees. Create a sense of policy ownership among employees by holding e-policy training sessions. Explain why the company has created the e-policies and what you and the rest of the management team expect from the staff. Create an environment in which employees feel free to ask questions about the organization's electronic policies.

Chapter 9 Recap and E-Action Plan: Minding Your Electronic Manners

1. To reduce the likelihood of offending readers, enforce clear netiquette guidelines for employees and managers.

2. Remind employees that the best way to control risk is to control content.

3. Use your employee netiquette policy to outlaw offensive remarks and prohibit behavior contrary to the organization's other HR/employee policies.

4. Use your netiquette policy to reinforce the dangers of hidden readers, attachments, and other risks.

5. Remind managers of the important role one-on-one business relationships play, even in the age of e-mail.

6. Conduct manager-specific training to limit the likelihood of workplace lawsuits.

Internet Policy Considerations
Keeping Employees in Line While They're Online

When employees make inappropriate use of the Internet, the result is waste.

Productive time is lost and computer assets wasted when employees spend hours monitoring stock market activity, bidding on merchandise at online auction sites, chatting with Internet friends, and just plain surfing the Net to see what's new.

Corporate reputations can be tarnished and legal defense funds tapped if employees' visits to pornographic sites lead to high-profile lawsuits that are covered by the media and dragged through the legal system for years.

Organizations can be driven out of business by the six-figure fines, software replacement costs, and lengthy periods of business interruption sometimes imposed by the software police when they are caught illegally downloading or duplicating copyrighted software.

Establish and Enforce a Comprehensive Internet Policy

As an employer, you are responsible for maintaining a harassment-free, discrimination-free, crime-free work environment. The development and implementation of a comprehensive Internet policy can help you accomplish that goal.

Ban Inappropriate Sites

Use your Internet policy to notify employees in writing that they are prohibited from using company computers to upload or download sexually explicit, violent, or otherwise objectionable images or language.

Prohibit the Wasting of Computer Resources

Use your Internet policy to drive home the point that employees are forbidden to waste the organization's computer resources. Remind employees that the company's Internet system is a business tool that should be used strictly for authorized commerce, communication, and research.

Outlaw wasteful activities such as surfing the Net for personal information, playing games online, visiting chat rooms, gambling, shopping, or engaging in any electronic activity that is not directly related to professional duties.

Enforce Language Guidelines

If you operate a bulletin board and/or chat room, be sure employees understand that the company's cyberlanguage guidelines apply to the Internet as well as e-mail (see Chapter 15).

Sample Online Language Statement
Employees are prohibited from posting or transmitting material that is obscene, hateful, harmful, malicious, threatening, hostile, abusive, vulgar, defamatory, profane, or racially, sexually, or ethnically objectionable.

Keep Web Copy Clean

Whether written by an outside consultant or an in-house writer, make sure your Web site copy is clean. Eager to fill white space, Web site copywriters sometimes will turn to the Internet or printed material for filler. Help your employees understand that it is illegal to use copyrighted materials without the express permission of the copyright holder. That includes copyrighted material downloaded from the Internet. (See Chapters 3 and 11.)

To avoid legal problems, it is a good idea to have your lawyer review your Web site copy for copyright and trademark clearance.

Apply the ABCs of Effective Electronic Writing

Whether it is an e-mail message or Internet copy, every document your employees produce reflects upon the professionalism and credibility of your operation. You may be an industry leader with a tremendous story to tell, but a Web site full of typos, mechanical errors, and awkward language will turn visitors away before they have the opportunity to learn what you have to offer.

Develop and enforce an organizationwide electronic writing policy to help speed the writing process and create consistency in your organization's documents (see Part 4). Assign an in-house editor or outside consultant the job of proofreading and editing all Internet and Intranet copy for mechanical correctness and appropriate style. Don't go online with copy that is anything less than a glowing reflection of your organization's professionalism.

Battle Technological Challenges with Technological Solutions

Don't take chances with Internet policy compliance. Back up your written Internet usage guidelines with monitoring and filtering software. Monitoring software provides a record of how employees are using the Internet and what sites they are visiting. Filtering software blocks access to prohibited sites. Both types of software can be programmed to alert you when an employee attempts to enter an outlawed site or devotes an excessive amount of time to Internet surfing.

The Internet is forever changing, and new software technologies are constantly under development. Software that gives you a terrific risk-management boost today may be totally inadequate for your needs six months from now. Work with your chief information officer to periodically review your organization's monitoring and filtering capabilities, and upgrade as necessary.

Train, Train, and Train Some More

As you begin to implement your organization's Internet policy, you will face some challenges. For many organizations, e-policies are totally new concepts that will take some getting used to. Employees who are ignorant of electronic risks will need to be educated about e-problems before they can be expected to embrace e-solutions.

In addition, many employees tend to view the Internet as an entertaining, freewheeling, anything-goes environment—not a business tool. Your challenge is to change their perception, to make those employees understand that the company's computers and Internet system exist for the company's benefit. Period.

The key to employee compliance is education. Reinforce your thoughtful, well-written Internet policy with ongoing training (see Part 5) and you will be on your way toward developing a low-risk electronic office.

Chapter 10 Recap and E-Action Plan: Keeping Online Activity on Track

1. Establish a policy that prohibits employees from using company computer assets to visit inappropriate sites or to upload or download objectionable material from the Internet.

2. Clearly communicate the fact that the organization's computer resources are not to be wasted, but are to be used for approved business purposes only.

3. Enforce cyberlanguage and content guidelines designed to keep Net copy clean and clear.

4. Don't leave compliance to chance. Back up your Internet policy with monitoring and filtering software.

5. Don't expect your employees to train themselves. Reinforce your Internet policy with ongoing employee education.

Software Policy Considerations
Don't Let Software Pirates Sink Your Ship

Would you walk into your local computer store and steal a package of software for business or personal use? Of course not. Yet many people who would never consider shoplifting from a retail store are guilty of "softlifting," or pirating, computer software.[1]

What is software piracy? Simply put, it is the unauthorized duplication and use of licensed computer software. Software piracy poses a unique challenge to the software industry and to employers. Unlike audiotapes and videotapes, which tend to lose quality with each duplication, computer software can be copied repeatedly with almost no impact on quality. For little or no cost, any computer user can produce thousands of copies of software that may have taken years of effort and millions of dollars to develop.

Software piracy can take place at the office or in the home. Copyright laws apply equally, regardless of whether it is a $1000 project management program that a department head has illegally copied and distributed to dozens of employees or a $100 computer game that is licensed to one person, then copied and shared with half a dozen friends and family members.

According to the SPA Antipiracy Division of the Software and Information Industry Association (SIIA), software piracy takes a variety of forms and has developed a language of its own.

1. **Softlifting:** If you purchase software with a single-user license, then load it on multiple computers or servers, you are guilty of softlifting. Individuals who copy and share software with friends and family members are softlifters. So are executives, managers, department heads, and employees who copy software for use by co-workers, independent contractors, clients, or other parties who are not licensed to use it.

2. **Counterfeiting:** Individuals who illegally produce, distribute, and/or sell software that is made to look like the real thing are known as software counterfeiters. How can you tell the difference between legitimate and counterfeit software? As a rule, if a software deal looks too good to be true, it probably is.

3. **Renting:** The unauthorized selling of software for temporary use is called *renting.* It also is illegal.

4. **Original equipment manufacturer (OEM) unbundling:** Unscrupulous distributors sometimes sell software that has been unbundled, or separated, from the hardware with which it was intended to be sold. Never purchase software that does not come with complete documentation, including registration papers and a user manual. That paperwork is your proof that the deal is legitimate.

5. **Uploading and downloading:** Software piracy extends to the Internet as well as programs copied onto disks and CDs. While it may be easy, it is illegal to upload or download copyrighted software from the Internet or bulletin boards without permission from the copyright owner.

6. **Hard disk loading:** It is illegal to install unauthorized copies of software onto the hard disks of personal computers. Dealers sometimes do this in order to create an incentive for consumers to purchase hardware. [2]

Software Piracy in the Workplace

In business situations, software piracy typically takes three forms.

Often an employer or employee will buy a piece of software with a single-user license, then load it onto multiple computers throughout the office. Perhaps your organization hasn't adequately budgeted for the software needs of all employees and a department head decides to copy programs in order to stretch dollars and complete assignments. Maybe your employees, eager for the flexibility of telecommuting, opt to download corporate software onto their home computers. Possibly a client, eager for all suppliers to use the same software, has provided your organization with one licensed copy and instructions to share it with everyone on the project team.

Whatever the reason, it is illegal and unethical to duplicate software that is licensed for single use. Employers who get caught with pirated software on their premises often pay a high price for what can be a very costly mistake. The fines for illegal software use run as high as $150,000 per title infringed. Multiply $150,000 times every employee in your office and you could be looking at a staggering sum. Add the cost of buying replacement software for each employee's computer, and it's no surprise that a company sued for copyright infringement easily could face a six- to seven-figure bill. That's ironic, considering that some organizations mistakenly view software piracy as a means to stretch their budgets.

Second, employees who bring software into the office from home also contribute to the piracy problem. Employees who think they are doing their colleagues and company a favor by supplying duplicated software may, in fact, be creating a legal problem that could cost everyone their job.

Third, downloading copyrighted software, clip art, fonts, and music from the Internet or bulletin boards also gets businesses into trouble. An employee who downloads software without securing permission from the copyright holder may save the organization time and money in the short run, but that short-term fix can prove very costly in terms of lost productivity, fines, defense costs, and negative publicity should the software police pay a visit.

Softlifters Will Be Prosecuted

Think the software police are a joke? They're not. Software piracy is an expensive problem, both for the software manufacturers who lose money every time a title is copied illegally and for the employers who face civil or criminal consequences if caught with pirated programs in the workplace.

How pervasive is software piracy? In the United States alone, one out of every four business software applications is pirated. Worldwide, software piracy accounted for $12 billion in lost revenue for software manufacturers in 1999.[3] This loss is solely attributed to organizations using business software illegally.

Fed up with costly theft, the software industry and federal government are getting tough with pirates. Software piracy is a federal offense. If suspected of using unlicensed software, you are likely to be visited by U.S. marshals and representatives of the SPA Antipiracy division of the Software & Information Industry Association (SIIA) or the Business Software Alliance (BSA). Acting on a whistle-blower's tip, the SIIA or BSA can obtain a court order, raid your organization, audit your software usage, and assess heavy fines.

Both the SIIA and BSA operate on tips called into their toll-free software piracy hotlines or sent electronically to their online hotlines. These hotlines, which generally field tips from disgruntled employees and vengeful former employees, have paid off for the software industry. Since 1993, the BSA has collected over $44 million in software piracy settlements.[4] The SPA Antipiracy hotline and Web site generate over 200 tips a week. Since 1995, SPA Antipiracy has acted on more than 2000 cases involving the illegal copying of software products published by SIIA member companies.[5]

The High Cost of Software Piracy

If found guilty of using illegally copied software, your organization could face enormous fines. If sued for civil copyright infringement, the penalty is up to $150,000 per title infringed. If charged with criminal violation, the fine is up to $250,000 per title infringed and up to five years imprisonment.[6]

Even cooperative companies are likely to end up with fines that cost the organization far more than it would have cost to buy new software in the first place. The high cost of software piracy really starts to add up when you calculate the cost of buying replacement software, the sting of negative publicity, and the havoc wreaked by virus-infected software, which is a common problem with pirated software.

Educate Employees about the Dangers of Workplace Piracy

The proliferation of software piracy may be due, in part, to ignorance. Employees and managers may not realize it is a crime to copy licensed software. Some employee-pirates actually may view themselves as corporate heroes, saving the organization dollars by copying software. Other employees may be unaware that one does not "own" software, one merely owns a license to use a software title.

Regardless of the reason for duplicating licensed software, it is wrong legally and morally. And it is the employer, not the individual pirate, who will be held legally and financially responsible should unlicensed software be uncovered in the course of a mandatory software audit.

Employers who want to avoid a run-in with the software police should take a three-pronged approach to prevention: (1) educate employees and managers about software piracy; (2) establish and maintain a firm antipiracy stance; and (3) incorporate a software usage policy into the organization's overall e-policy.

The benefits of establishing a software usage policy include protecting your organization from piracy-related litigation, insulating your computers from defective software that could introduce viruses into your network, and reducing the overall costs of software usage.

Software Usage Checklist for Employers

While employees contribute significantly to the presence of illegal software in the workplace, employers are held responsible for software violations. The best advice for employers: Monitor and manage employees' software use before you face a time-consuming and costly lawsuit, stiff fines, or the loss of valuable data courtesy of virus-laden software. Here are some guidelines for employers who want to keep the workplace free from software piracy.[7]

Adopt an Antipiracy Stance

Make it clear to employees that your organization does not condone the illegal duplication of software and will not tolerate it. Violation of the organization's software usage policy will lead to disciplinary action or termination.

Review Copyright Law with Employees

From the moment of its creation, software automatically is protected by federal copyright law. Purchasing a license for a copy of software does not give you the right to make additional copies without permission of the copyright owner. The licensee is allowed to copy the software onto a single computer and make one backup copy for archival purposes. That's it.

The rules are simple. You must purchase a new software package for every computer on which a given program will run. No software, fonts, clip art, or music may be downloaded from the Internet without permission from the copyright holder. It also is illegal to rent, lease, or lend original copies of software without permission of the copyright owner.

Audit Your Organization's Computers

Determine what software is available on each computer workstation and what licenses you own to support the software used. If you find illegal copies, destroy them and buy new software before the software police order you to do so. The time and money you invest in replacing illegal software will be a fraction of the productivity and financial loss you would experience if the SIIA or BSA catch you operating with pirated software.

Educate Managers and Department Heads

Managers should understand the organization's software costs, needs, and risks. Teach managers to treat software like any other business asset. Budget for it, and take appropriate action, as detailed in your software usage policy, against employee-pirates.

Teach Employees the Lingo of Pirates

To Internet insiders, "warez" means pirated or illegal software. In general, the standard in the Internet community is to create plural words that describe illegal activity by using the letter *z instead of s*. Notify employees that software or sites labeled "warez" usually contain illegal material and should be avoided and reported to the organization's chief information officer.

Recognize the Hidden Costs of Software Piracy

Stolen software comes with no guarantees and no technical support. If you develop a problem or become infected with a computer virus, you are on your own. The solution to your problem could end up costing you more than licensed software would have cost in the first place. Make sure managers and employees understand that the few dollars they save by copying software today could wind up costing the company hundreds of thousands of dollars tomorrow in fines and replacement costs.

Document Software Purchases

Attach copies of purchase orders to licenses. Register all software with its manufacturer. Appoint one employee or department to track and record the organization's software purchases and use.

Watch for Illegally Bundled Software

If a reseller offers you a computer system that's bundled with numerous copies of popular software programs, check to see if all the software comes complete with full documentation, including license agreements, original disks, manuals, and registration cards. If not, run away from this "deal."

Understand Your License Agreements

Software usually includes specific license provisions that allow for the use of programs at work, home, or on your organization's computer network. If you are confused about what a license covers, call the software manufacturer and ask.

Remove Temptation

If employees' software needs exceed your organization's supply, fix the problem. Purchase needed software before employees, eager for a quick fix, start to copy programs.

Enforce Your Efforts

To be effective, your organization's antipiracy efforts must be communicated clearly and consistently. Institute a program of continuing education for managers and employees. Conduct periodic audits. Make the retention of documentation mandatory. Put teeth in your self-policing program by consistently enforcing penalties for violators.

Manager's Tip Sheet: Answers to Employees' Most Common Software Piracy Questions

To help facilitate the smooth and effective introduction of your software usage policy, you may want to provide managers with a list of the questions employees are most likely to ask during the first days, weeks, and perhaps months following the introduction of your organization's software policy. A sample question and answer sheet, developed with the assistance of the Software & Information Industry Association,[8] follows.

Q. Who polices software piracy in the workplace?

A. Two trade associations enforce software copyrights and trademarks for software publishers and information content providers. They are the Software and Information Industry Association (SIIA) SPA Antipiracy Division and the Business Software Alliance (BSA).

Q. Exactly what is software piracy?

A. Software piracy is the unauthorized use of software. Types of software piracy include the following: (1) Purchasing a single-user license, then loading the software onto multiple computers or a server. This is called *softloading*. (2) Making, distributing, and/or selling copies that appear to be from an authorized source. This is called *counterfeiting*. (3) Renting software without permission from the copyright holder. (4) Distributing and/or selling software that has been unbundled, or separated, from the products with which it was intended to have been bundled. (5) Downloading copyrighted software from the Internet or bulletin boards without permission from the copyright holder.

Q. I came across inexpensive software at a weekend show at my local civic center. Is it legitimate software?

A. It may be legitimate software, such as shareware, but it may be illegal. If illegal, it is likely to be counterfeit or unbundled. Unbundled software often is labeled "not for resale." Use caution. Do not bring this type of questionable software, or any personal software for that matter, into the office. If the deal seems too good to be true, contact the toll-free antipiracy hotline operated by the SIIA's SPA Antipiracy Division (800/388-7478 or www.siia.net/piracy) or the BSA (888/667-4722 or www.bsa.org).

Q. What is shareware?

A. Shareware is software that is freely distributed for evaluation purposes only. Typically, the evaluation period is 30 days. If you wish to keep a shareware software program after the 30-day trial, you must then purchase your evaluation copy.

Q. Why shouldn't I use pirated software? Who am I hurting by doing so?

A. First of all, it is illegal. Second, it is risky. Unless you are certain that your software comes from an authorized source, you could get a program that is infected with a virus, is incompatible, or is not fully functioning. Since pirated software doesn't come with a manual or technical support, you have no recourse when it fails. Third, you may be hurting yourself or the organization by failing to take advantage of the economic benefits of newer software licenses. Fourth, there won't be another version of your favorite software if manufacturers, hurt by software theft, do not have the revenue to reinvest in research and development. Fifth, software piracy is unethical. Put yourself in the shoes of the software author and consider how you would feel if your time and talent were stolen.

Finally, if you value your job, don't pirate software. The organization's software usage policy prohibits the use of pirated software. Violate the policy and you will face disciplinary action and possible termination.

Q. I have seen the same copy of a software package run on multiple computers. There are no licenses or disks. Is this piracy?

A. Yes. Any single-user copy of software run on multiple computers without licenses or disks is pirated. If the license states that the software can be used on only one computer or by one person, then using it multiple times is a violation of the license agreement.

If you notice this happening in the office, bring the situation to the attention of your supervisor or the CIO immediately.

Q. Are fonts and clip art copyrighted?

A. Yes. Both fonts and clip art are copyrighted and are protected under the same law as software. In addition, the liabilities are the same. That means each pirated font or clip art image could result in damages of up to $150,000 per item infringed. If an outside software audit were to uncover pirated software loaded onto the computers of just a dozen employees, the organization could face fines up to $1.2 million. Add to that the cost of buying replacement software and you can see how quickly the cost of piracy can mount.

Q. I bought a home computer with a lot of software already on the hard drive. I don't have a license or disk for it. What should I do? Is that piracy?

A. If software you bought did not come with a license or registration, it probably is pirated. Owning it puts you at risk. You have an illegal product on your PC, and it may contain viruses that could crash your hard drive. If a dealer sells you software with no paperwork, return it and report the incident to SIIA's SPA Antipiracy Division (800/388-7478 or www.spa.org/piracy) or the BSA (888/667-4722 or www.bsa.org).

Of course, software may be installed legally on a computer. Generally referred to as *bundled*, this software is specially licensed to the computer with which it came. If you have a question about the software's legality, consult the reseller or the publisher of the product.

Q. I visited a store that was renting computer games and software. Is that piracy?

A. Maybe. It is illegal to rent software without written permission from the copyright holder. When in doubt, ask the rental store manager to show you the permission, or license, to rent the product. If the manager can't produce the license, the store probably is not authorized to rent the product and is guilty of piracy.

Q. If I find software available for download on the Internet, should I assume I can do so legally?

A. Not necessarily. In general, there are three types of software: shareware, freeware, and commercial. You may legally download shareware or freeware. Commercial software is not legally available for download on the Internet. If you have questions, check with the publisher of the software to determine if the distributor, or the operator of the site, has a license to distribute commercial software.

Q. My home computer server operator allows me to download software free as part of my account. Is this legal?

A. Possibly. Many server operators have licenses with publishers to distribute software to their subscribers. Sometimes, they make shareware and freeware available to their subscribers to test and use if they wish. If you have concerns that pirated software may be available, check with your server operator or the publisher to confirm appropriate licensing.

Q. Is it illegal to link to pirated software?

A. It may be. Under certain circumstances, links to illegal material such as pirated software may represent a contributory infringement under copyright law. In addition, aiding someone in committing an infringement is unethical and violates the sanctity of the Internet community.

Q. What are "warez"?

A. Sites labeled "warez" usually contain pirated software. Members of the Internet community typically signal illegal activity by using the letter z instead of s to create plural words. Avoid these sites.

Q. Is it illegal to post serial numbers and cracker utilities?

A. The posting of serial numbers and cracker utilities to circumvent copyright protections in software may represent contributory infringement under copyright law, when used by an individual to commit a direct infringement.

Q. If I know of pirated software within my organization's system, should I file a piracy report with SIIA's SPA Antipiracy Division or the BSA?

A. No. Give management the opportunity to investigate first and respond to the problem on its own, according to the guidelines spelled out in the software usage policy. If, based on your confidential tip, management uncovers illegal software in the system, it will remove, destroy, and replace it with legal software. If the party or parties responsible for the violation(s) can be identified, appropriate disciplinary action will be taken.

Q. What would happen if the SIIA's SPA Antipiracy Division were to get wind of the existence of pirated software within our organization?

A. A report, typically based on a tip from an employee or ex-employee, would be investigated to confirm its validity. If the report were valid, one of four actions would be taken: (1) a cease and desist letter would be sent; (2) a cooperative audit would be conducted; (3) litigation would be initiated; or (4) additional information would be gathered.

Q. What happens when a suspect company tries to destroy evidence of piracy?

 A. SPA Antipiracy can file a lawsuit if there is good reason to believe a company may destroy evidence. A company that destroys software after a lawsuit is filed may be in contempt of court and could face disciplinary action in addition to the copyright infringement claim.

Q. Is there a reward for reporting piracy?

A. No. The trade associations that enforce software copyrights do not offer monetary rewards. Rewards would compromise the integrity of reports and the credibility of tipsters.

Q. What type of fines are imposed on software pirates?

A. If sued for copyright infringement, the penalty is up to $100,000 per title infringed. If charged with a criminal violation, the fine is up to $250,000 per title infringed and up to five years imprisonment.

Q. How can the company prove its software has been purchased legally?

A. To demonstrate copyright compliance, SPA Antipiracy requires positive proof that all software has been purchased. The best proof includes approved purchase orders, invoices, product-specific licenses, vendor/reseller reports, and canceled checks. Other documentation provided by the company may be accepted at SPA Antipiracy's discretion. Normally, original media (CD-ROMs, diskettes, manuals, etc.) are not accepted documentation.

Q. Does a company's software usage policy shield it from liability?

A. No. Having all employees review and sign a copy of the company's software usage policy is part of a comprehensive effort to shape employee conduct and reduce the risk of workplace liability. In spite of the existence of a written software policy, the company would be liable if found with illegal software on employees' computers.

Q. If I know of a department head who is distributing pirated software to employees and I don't report the piracy, am I liable?

A. Not in the eyes of SPA Antipiracy. It holds the company, not the individual employee, responsible. You would, however, be guilty of violating the company's written software usage policy—assuming it had one—were you to fail to bring this situation to management's attention.

Q. I have some old software at home that I no longer use. I want to give it away. Do I need special permission?

A. It depends on what you mean by "old software." If, for example, you wish to give away old software that has been upgraded, the answer generally is no. Upgrade licenses supplant the license of the original, voiding the original license and making the original version legally unusable.

On the other hand, if you bought a new, full copy of a higher version of the software, license permitting, you could sell or give away the older version.

Q. I would like to use a software program on my home computer, but the publishing company has gone out of business. Is it okay for me to make a copy since it no longer is producing this software for purchase?

A. Copyright may be valid for 75 years or more, long after a publisher has gone out of business. Copyrights may even be transferred or assigned to someone else. To copy a software program, you need express permission from the copyright holder. The U.S. Copyright Office may be able to help you find the current copyright holder, so you could write for permission to copy the product.

Q. When I purchase software for home use, what paperwork should I expect to accompany it?

A. A reputable dealer will sell software complete with the original disks, manuals, registration card, and the license agreement. If these items are not made available, do not buy the product.

Chapter 11 Recap and E-Action Plan: Police Yourself before the Software Police Come Knocking on Your Door

1. As an employer, you cannot afford to ignore software piracy or dismiss it as insignificant. Adopt a strict antipiracy stance and enforce it consistently.

2. Develop a comprehensive training program for employees. Make it clear that softlifting is a serious crime that can trigger stiff penalties for the company and put employees' jobs at risk.

3. Make sure managers, supervisors, and department heads understand what software piracy is and why it is important for the organization to assume a zero-tolerance posture regarding piracy. In particular, managers who traditionally have viewed software piracy as a victimless crime, a relatively harmless way to stretch a departmental budget, need to be educated about the risks inherent in software piracy.

4. Do not assume employees know anything about software piracy or the laws regarding copyright infringement. Prepare managers to provide "*Software Piracy 101*" training for employees. Specifically, arm managers and trainers with a comprehensive tip sheet that answers the questions employees are most likely to ask about legal and illegal software use.

PART

four

Establishing an

Electronic Writing

Policy for Employees

E-Writing Guidelines Ensure Speedy—and Safe—Communication

Want to facilitate compliance with your organization's e-policies? One of the most effective ways to do so is to incorporate electronic writing guidelines into your comprehensive e-policy. Use your e-writing policy to help employees produce acceptable and effective e-mail messages and Internet copy.

Whether sending e-mail messages, publishing an electronic newsletter, drafting copy for the organization's Internet or Intranet site, or posting copy to a bulletin board—whatever an employee's e-communication challenge might be—the organization's electronic writing policy would apply. Your e-writing policy will give employees writing rules to work by, while helping speed the composition process for those who might otherwise get bogged down in questions of mechanics or issues of style.

Assessing and Addressing Employees' Electronic Writing Needs

As a precursor to establishing your e-writing policy, it is a good idea to determine what most confuses and concerns your employees about electronic business writing. You also will want to poll managers for their insights into your staff's overall writing capabilities.

The ability to write clear, compelling, traditional business documents will determine an employee's ability to compose effective electronic documents. Have employees participate in a writing self-assessment to determine their attitudes toward electronic writing and identify their writing strengths and weaknesses. Use the information gleaned from your survey to structure an electronic writing policy that best meets the needs of your employees and your organization as a whole.

Managerial Writing Review

Before surveying employees about their electronic writing skills, it is advisable to seek the input of managers and supervisors. The people who work with the staff daily and are exposed to their writing on a regular basis are well positioned to address the organization's overall writing strengths and weaknesses.

Since you will be relying on your management team to help enforce the organization's e-writing policy, it is important to unveil the project to them and secure their support before introducing employees to the electronic writing skills survey and policy.

Your managerial writing review could combine a written questionnaire with group discussion to encourage managers to give thoughtful consideration to the organization's electronic and traditional writing needs and problems.

Sample E-Writing Questionnaire for Managers

1. Across the board, what are the biggest writing problems (electronic and traditional) facing our employees?

   _____

   _____

2. How effective are the letters, memos, and other documents employees send via e-mail?
   ___Very ___Somewhat ___Minimally ___Not Effective
   at All

3. How much time do you spend editing and rewriting employee e-mail and other business correspondence?
___None ___Small Amount of Time ___Considerable Amount of Time

4. In terms of copy (content, writing style, and mechanical correctness), what is your opinion of the organization's Internet site, Intranet site, and e-mail newsletter?

_____

_____

5. Do you think it would it be beneficial to bring a professional writing coach on board to help employees polish their business writing skills (electronic and traditional) and brush up on the do's and don'ts of netiquette?   ___Yes ___No

6. Would you appreciate taking a business writing refresher yourself?   ___Yes ___No

7. Do you require members of your department to use a specific writing style manual?   ___Yes ___No

8. If the answer to question 7 is yes, what style manual do you use?

_____

_____

9. Do you require members of your department to use a specific dictionary?   ___Yes ___No

10. If the answer to question 9 is yes, what dictionary do you use?

_____

_____

11. Do you expect much resistance from employees toward the organization's electronic writing policy?   ___Yes ___No

12. Do you have any concerns about enforcing the organization's electronic writing policy?   ___**Yes** ___**No**

13. If the answer to question 12 is yes, what concerns do you have?

_____

_____

14. What can management do to ensure the smooth, successful adoption of the organization's electronic writing policy?

_____

_____

Understanding Employees' Electronic Writing Concerns

Once you have completed your management writing review, your next step will be to survey employees about their electronic writing strengths, weaknesses, questions, and concerns. To ensure honest responses and maximum participation, conduct the survey anonymously. Have a senior executive (the more senior the better) announce the survey and elicit employee participation.

A sample announcement memo and employee survey follow.

Sample E-Writing Survey Memo

Date:	**April 20, 2001**
To:	**All Employees**
From:	**Matt Kennedy, President and CEO, XYZ Corporation**
Subject:	**E-Mail, Internet, and Software Usage Questionnaire**

As part of the organization's overall e-policy initiative, we will be developing electronic writing guidelines to help employees maximize the effectiveness and appropriateness of e-mail messages and Internet copy. To that end, we are asking all employees to complete the attached Electronic Writing Skills Survey.

This is an anonymous survey. We won't even ask your name. All we ask is that you answer the questions thoughtfully and turn in your completed questionnaire by April 9.

Most questions require a true/false or yes/no answer. In only a few instances are you required to give a more detailed response. If you are unfamiliar with any of the terms used ("smiley," for example), indicate that by checking "Don't know."

You have until April 9 to deposit your completed questionnaire in the Electronic Writing Skills Survey dropoff box located outside the entrance to the employee cafeteria. Thank you for your help in making the company's e-writing policy as effective and successful as possible.

Sample Electronic Writing Skills Survey

1. Because e-mail is intended, and expected, to be a quick means of communication, the rules of grammar, punctuation, and style do not apply.
   ___True ___False ___Don't Know

2. E-mail readers tend to be more forgiving of writing errors than readers of traditional business documents.
   ___True ___False ___Don't Know

3. Do you electronically spell-check every e-mail message before sending it out? ___Yes ___No

4. Do you manually proofread every e-mail message before sending it out? ___Yes ___No

5. If unclear on the spelling or meaning of a word, do you always take time to look it up in the dictionary before finalizing electronic copy? ___Yes ___No

6. Is your electronic writing consistently free of sexist language?
   ___Yes ___No ___Don't Know

7. To capture the reader's attention and communicate the importance of your e-mail message, it is a good idea to write e-mail messages entirely in uppercase (capital) letters.

___True ___False ___Don't Know

8. Do you use smileys to express emotion in business-related e-mail messages?

___Yes ___No ___Don't Know

9. If you answered yes to question 8, how often do you use smileys?

___Always ___Occasionally ___Never

10. Please draw the smiley you most often use in business e-mail and explain what it means.

_____

_____

11. Why do you use smileys? Under what circumstances would you add a smiley to a business-related e-mail message?

_____

_____

12. Has a business reader ever questioned the meaning of one of your smileys? ___Yes ___No

13. Short sentences indicate intellectual weakness. Long, heavily punctuated sentences are more likely to impress readers.

___Yes ___No ___Don't Know

14. It is a good idea to save the most important information for the end of your e-mail message. That gives the reader an incentive to read the message through to the end.

___True ___False ___Don't Know

15. It is a good idea to put the most important information at the beginning of your e-mail message.

___True ___False ___Don't Know

16. Writing a powerful subject line will improve the likelihood that your e-mail message will be opened and read.
___**True** ___**False** ___**Don't Know**

17. Do you keep a writing style manual on your desk and refer to it when you have questions about grammar, punctuation, or other mechanical issues? ___**Yes** ___**No**

18. If you answered yes to question 17, what writing style manual(s) do you use?

_____

_____

19. Are your confident of your ability to punctuate correctly? ___**Yes** ___**No**

20. Are you confident of your ability to use proper grammar? ___**Yes** ___**No**

21. When sending e-mail to a reader in another country, you don't have to worry about language barriers. After all, English is the international language of commerce.
___**True** ___**False** ___**Don't Know**

22. Do you know the difference between the active voice and the passive voice? ___**Yes** ___**No**

23. If the answer to question 22 is yes, does your writing tend to be active or passive?
___**Active** ___**Passive**

24. Do you ever ask anyone within the company to proofread or edit your writing? ___**Yes** ___**No**

25. If the answer to question 24 is yes, on whom do you rely for editorial assistance? Please provide either the name or title of your unofficial editor.

_____

_____

26. What do you consider to be your greatest writing
problem?

_____

_____

27. What do you feel is your greatest writing strength?

_____

_____

Putting Your E-Writing Findings to Work

Assign responsibility for the e-writing surveys, both manager and
employee versions, to a member of your e-policy team or an outside
writing coach. The responsible individual will develop your writing
questionnaires, conduct management discussions, and draft a report
based on managers' and employees' responses.

The e-writing report, recapping employees' writing strengths and
weaknesses, will help shape your customized electronic writing policy. Along with your internal research, feel free to adopt the material
contained in Chapters 13 through 16 to create a powerful electronic
writing policy for your organization.

Chapter 12 Recap and E-Action Plan: Designing an E-Writing Policy That Meets Employee Needs

1. Enforce electronic content by imposing an electronic writing policy.

2. Before drafting your e-writing policy, survey managers and
   employees to determine their electronic and traditional writing
   strengths and weaknesses.

3. Couple your written managerial writing review with group discussion. Instill in managers a sense of ownership of the e-writing policy.

4. Conduct the employees' electronic writing skills survey in an
   anonymous, nonthreatening manner.

Powerful and Persuasive, Safe and Secure Electronic Writing

In the course of the average business day, e-mail users may receive dozens, even hundreds, of messages. Web sites may welcome thousands, possibly millions, of visitors. With all that online traffic, the battle to capture and hold the attention and interest of the electronic reader is fierce.

At heart, the electronic writer's job is persuasion. Whether an employee is trying to convince an e-mail recipient to attend a meeting, convert Web site visitors into buyers, or persuade e-newsletter readers to subscribe, the writer's goal is to motivate the reader to act. Fortunately, business writers have in their arsenal certain tools that can help enhance the overall power and persuasiveness of their electronic writing.[1]

Writing a Subject Line with Real Oomph

E-mail writers can increase the likelihood of messages being read and retained, rather than ignored and deleted, by writing compelling, descriptive subject lines. In general, a recipient's electronic mailbox will display only a brief subject line for each message. By disregarding the important role the subject line plays in motivating readers, writers often compose subject lines that are too vague and uninspired to be effective.

Fortunately, with just a bit of thought and a little effort, electronic business writers can learn to write subject lines that will make their e-mail messages stand out. Use your e-writing policy to teach employees how to write powerful subject lines. Here are some pointers:

1. State your message clearly, concisely, and descriptively. An effective subject line should draw the reader into the message and communicate subject matter before the message itself is opened and read.

   For example, a subject line that reads "Network Failure" lacks the impact of "Hackers Launch DOS Attack." In just four words, the more descriptive subject line alerts readers that malicious hackers have successfully launched a denial of service attack, shutting down at least one network operation. Thanks to this vivid subject line, the e-mail message practically screams to be opened and read by readers concerned about cybercrime.

2. Consider the primary audience when writing the subject line, but don't overdo it. Resist the urge to incorporate technical terms, acronyms, or industry jargon into subject lines. The writer's job is to entice readers to open messages, not scare them away before they start reading.

3. Remember the hidden reader. When e-mail messages are forwarded from one reader to the next, the original subject line often is left intact. A well-planned subject line will enable the writer to attract, or repel, unintended readers. Before sending a message, consider whether or not the subject line will retain its effectiveness should the message land on the screens of unintended readers.

4. Don't use the subject line to oversell a message or trick the reader into opening a document. A reader may fall for a mislead-

ing subject line once, but the next message the writer sends might be ignored, or simply deleted before it is read.

5. When the occasion calls for it, write a subject line that appeals to multiple audiences. What's the most effective way to motivate a group of people with varying needs and interests to open and read a single e-mail message? Compose a subject line with mass appeal.

Let's say a supervisor instructs an employee to send an e-mail message inviting members of the creative services and information systems departments to the demonstration of a new graphic design software package. If the writer composes a subject line that reads, "Graphic Design Software Demo," those in the information systems department likely will assume the meeting does not pertain to them and will delete the message without reading it. If, on the other hand, the subject line reads, "Tech Solutions to Graphics," the graphic designers and other creatives are likely to be scared off.

The solution: Write an inclusive subject line that appeals to both audiences. "Art and Tech Software Demo" might draw a crowd from both departments.

Grabbing and Holding the Electronic Reader's Attention

To maximize the impact of any document, electronic or traditional, start strong. The lead, which begins with the first word of sentence one and ends at the conclusion of the first paragraph, is the business writer's best (sometimes only) opportunity to grab the reader's attention. A well-conceived lead draws readers into the e-mail message, motivating them to read the document through to its conclusion.

A particularly important element of e-mail messages, a well-written lead will allow the reader to grasp the writer's meaning immediately, and decide whether to continue reading, save the document for later review, or delete it on the spot.

Whether it appears in an e-mail message, on a Web site, or in some other form of online writing, the lead performs several important roles. The lead structures the message, leaving the reader with no doubt why the document has been written or whether to continue reading it. The lead delivers the document's most important, compelling information right up front, often in the form of a conclusion. The lead summarizes what is to come later in the document. And if well written, the lead captures and holds the reader's attention.

Separating the Weak from the Strong

What distinguishes a strong, successful lead from a weak one? With no waste of the writer's words or reader's time, a strong lead tells readers what they need to know. A well-written lead enables even a rushed reader to grasp the message's meaning immediately. Here is an example of an effective lead:

> As of January 1, personal use of the company e-mail system is prohibited. First-time violators will be placed on immediate probation. Three violations will result in termination.

This lead leaves no room for misunderstanding. In twenty-eight words, employees learn what the new policy is and how violations will be handled. An employee who does not read beyond sentence one still would have a clear sense of what the message is about.

Conversely, the weak lead below contains too much unnecessary and secondary information. Not until the end of the paragraph does the reader learn that the company is instituting a tough new e-mail policy.

> Nearly two-thirds of XYZ Company's 1500 employees are using the company's e-mail system on a regular basis. Unfortunately, not all that e-mail correspondence is business-related. Many of our 1500 employees are using the e-mail system daily to send and receive personal messages. Management is aware of this situation and wants it stopped. As of January 1, the e-mail system at XYZ Company is reserved for business use. Any employee caught using the system for personal reasons will be put on probation following the first

offense. Three violations of the new e-mail policy will result in termination.

At almost 100 words, this lead is more than three times longer than the more streamlined and persuasive version. The misguided writer has taken a chance that recipients will read this bloated message through to the last three sentences, where the meat of the message resides.

Applying the Inverted Pyramid to Electronic Writing

Saving the best stuff, the primary message, for last may work fine in mystery novels, but it is no way to write a successful e-mail message—or any other electronic business document for that matter.

Effective electronic business writing should be structured as an inverted, or upside-down, pyramid. The most important information is communicated right up front in the lead. Following the lead, information is presented in descending order of importance.

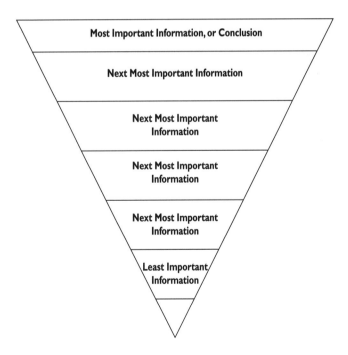

Don't Be a Mystery Writer

Writers can maximize the effectiveness of their e-mail messages by leading with the primary message, rather than saving the good stuff for the end. Writers cannot rely on busy e-mail recipients to read the entire message from beginning to end. Many readers merely scan a message's subject line and the opening sentence or two to determine whether or not the message warrants further attention.

To ensure e-mail documents are read and acted upon, state the primary message clearly, concisely, and as close to the beginning of the e-mail as possible. A writer who communicates persuasively in the first sentence of the first paragraph should have no difficulty capturing the reader's interest and attention for the remainder of the document.

Why an Inverted Pyramid Approach to E-Documents?

Deluged with electronic and traditional correspondence, few business people have time to read every memo, letter, and proposal that lands in their electronic mailboxes or crosses their desks. How does a harried reader decide which e-mail documents to read and respond to and which to delete from the screen? Typically, the reader scans the subject line and reads the lead to determine whether to continue reading or not. Writers who want their e-mail to succeed have no choice but to deliver the primary message right up front, at the beginning of the e-mail document.

Instruct employees to think about their goals before they start to write. Is the goal to alert readers to a problem? To notify staff of a rescheduled meeting? To persuade an executive to increase a departmental budget?

Whatever the objective, state it clearly, concisely, and as close to the beginning of the e-mail message as possible. Ideally, make the primary purpose known in the first sentence of the first paragraph of each e-mail message.

Sample Lead Written in Inverted Pyramid Style

XYZ Company prohibits the illegal copying of computer software, and any violation will result in immediate termination. Employees are prohibited from duplicating software that is licensed to the company. Employees are not allowed to bring software from home into the office. Employees also are prohibited from downloading copyrighted software from the Internet.

Analysis

Employees need read no further than sentence one to understand what the software policy is all about. Sentences two, three, and four merely expand on what has been stated, clearly, in the paragraph's opening sentence.

Sample Lead Written in Mystery Writer Style

Each year, the U.S. software industry loses billions of dollars to stolen, or pirated, software. Software piracy impacts manufacturers' revenues, costs employees their jobs, and lessens the likelihood of new software titles being introduced by financially strapped manufacturers. XYZ Company supports the software industry's efforts to stop piracy in its tracks. To that end, XYZ Company has established an employee software usage policy. Effective immediately, the illegal copying of computer software is prohibited. Employees are prohibited from duplicating software that is licensed to the company. Employees are not allowed to bring software from home into the office. And, employees are prohibited from downloading copyrighted software from the Internet. Any violation will result in immediate termination.

Analysis

Do your employees really care about the financial woes of software manufacturers and their employees? Doubtful. Your employees do, however, care about their own job security and financial future. Tell your employees what they want and need to know by trimming the first four, unnecessary sentences in this fat paragraph.

Moving to the Heart of the Message

A compelling subject line will help ensure an e-mail message is opened. A powerful lead will motivate the recipient to read the message immediately, or retain it for later review. Instruct employees to use the body of the message to add information (features, benefits, and details) that are of meaning to the reader and reinforce the lead's message.

Chapters 14 and 15 provide additional tips to help guide employees toward content that is clear, clean, and compliant.

Chapter 13 Recap and E-Action Plan: Enhancing the Overall Power and Persuasiveness of Electronic Writing

1. E-mail is intended as a quick means of communication. An e-writing policy will help speed the writing process and boost the confidence of employee-writers.

2. Focus on readability and accessibility when formatting your e-policies. Use your e-writing policy to teach employees how to format e-mail and Internet copy for maximum effectiveness.

3. Remind employees that electronic readers are busy readers. To ensure that e-mail is read and acted upon, e-writers should write powerful subject lines, start strong, and adhere to the inverted pyramid writing style.

The ABCs of Effective Electronic Business Writing

Whether composing an e-mail message or drafting copy for your organization's Web site or electronic newsletter, employees should adhere to the ABCs of effective business writing. In other words, electronic copy must be *accurate, brief,* and *clear* to be effective.[1]

Accuracy: Speedy Doesn't Mean Sloppy

Use the development of your organization's e-policies as an opportunity to stress the fact that every document employees write is a reflection of their individual professionalism and the organization's credibility. Most electronic readers are looking for any reason to disqualify or disregard e-mail messages, particularly sales pitches. Help your employees overcome readers' objections and accomplish corporate goals by instituting clear and consistent electronic writing guidelines.

Instruct employees to think about accuracy from the reader's perspective. If a writer cannot be relied on to construct an accurate one-page e-mail message, why should a prospective customer trust your organization to get the job done? If your organization's Web site is riddled with spelling slips and grammatical goofs, how can buyers rely on your products or services to perform as advertised?

Spelling Counts, Even in Cyberspace

Electronic communication may be quick, but it should not be careless. Prohibit employees from sending e-mail messages or posting Internet copy without first proofreading manually and spell-checking electronically. If there is any doubt about the spelling of a word or the accuracy of a statement, employees should take time to check. No e-mail message should be sent without first confirming the spelling of the recipient's name and title. Nothing irks readers more than having this information appear incorrectly in print.

People do pay attention to typos. It is not unusual for even the busiest reader to zero in on misspellings. In fact, some decision-makers go out of their way to locate spelling errors in business documents, electronic and traditional. Don't give readers any excuse to delete your organization's documents from the screen without taking time to read them in full. Spelling errors and typos undermine your organization's credibility and weaken the impact of individual e-mail messages. Proofreading is a tough but indispensable part of the electronic writing process. It should be required of all employees.

Five Electronic Spelling Tips

As part of your e-writing policy, share these five electronic spelling suggestions with employees.

1. Run all written documents through your electronic spell-checker software. Bear in mind, however, that spell-checker software cannot correct usage. For example, your spell checker cannot distinguish between "marshal" and "marshall," "it's" and "its," or "affect" and "effect." Proofread manually first, using the electronic tool for your final check.

2. Refer to a good, up-to-date dictionary. Keep a dictionary next to your computer workstation and refer to it whenever you are unsure of spelling or usage. The dictionary also is a valuable source of synonyms for writers who tend to use the same words time and again.

3. When you are in the writing groove, don't let spelling questions slow you down. Don't stop writing to look up or spell-check every word that strikes you as odd. Wait until you are finished writing your document; then go back to the beginning and proofread thoroughly.

4. Take plenty of time with important business documents. Once you push "send," your e-mail is on its way and probably cannot be retrieved. Never put in writing, electronic or traditional, anything that could come back to haunt you or the organization. E-mail may be instantaneous, but it is not invisible. If time allows, print a hard copy and proofread it before sending your electronic document into cyberspace.

5. Seek expert advice. Don't guess about grammar, punctuation, and writing style. The mistakes you make could have a negative impact on your career and the company's business relationships. Refer to the organization's electronic writing policy for insight into company-approved content and construction issues. Look up questionable words and frequently confused or misused words in the dictionary.

Brief Is Best: Trim the Fat from Electronic Writing

What's the primary benefit of electronic communication? Speed. E-mail facilitates quick and easy correspondence with colleagues, customers, and suppliers. The Internet enables buyers, investors, and prospective employees to check out the organization's capabilities and products instantaneously.

For best results, instruct employees to keep their words, sentences, and paragraphs lean. The result: Electronic documents will be much easier to write, read, and comprehend.

As a rule, e-mail messages should be restricted to one screen page. If a subject warrants additional copy, then the writer should supply that information in the form of an attachment. When using an attachment, make the e-mail message itself a one-page executive summary of the material contained in the attachment. Use the message to persuade the reader to open and read the lengthier document.

Unlike e-mail, electronic newsletters and e-zines promoting your organization's products and services may call for multiple screen pages. Certainly, your Web site will consist of several pages, each devoted to a different aspect of your business or a specific product offering. Regardless of the document, all electronic writing should be succinct and persuasive. In short, e-documents should be easy to read and act upon.

Aim for Simplicity

To maximize the effectiveness of electronic copy, instruct employees to keep their writing short and simple. In business writing, there is no prize given for the longest word. Readers seldom are impressed by big words. On the contrary, unfamiliar words tend to confuse and irritate readers, making the goal of persuasion difficult to achieve. Electronic writers can do themselves and their readers a favor by selecting words that are short, descriptive, and familiar. Readers will thank the writer for doing so.

Likewise, short sentences are preferable to long ones. Short sentences are easier to write, read, and understand. Long sentences, often challenging, are particularly difficult to read on screen. Long sentences also tend to bury ideas.

Furthermore, long sentences test the writer's ability to use grammar and punctuation correctly. A hurried e-mail reader is more likely to delete a confusing, error-filled message than to take time to correct the writer's mechanical errors and decipher the document's meaning. Instruct employees to put short sentences to work, communicating the primary message clearly, right from the beginning of the electronic document.

Strive for an Active Style

Unsure how to trim the fat from sentences without sacrificing meaning? One of the best ways to streamline electronic communication is to write documents in the active voice. Not only does the active voice have more energy than the passive, it requires fewer words. Simply switching from a passive to an active construction will guarantee sentences are shorter, more readable, and more powerful.

Instruct employees who have trouble understanding what constitutes the active voice simply to ask, "Who is doing what to whom?" Then have the employee write the sentence, focusing on who (the actor), what (the action), and whom (the object being acted upon).

Tip: In an active construction, the actor, or subject, always appears before the action, or verb. When the actor follows the action, that is a telltale sign of a passive sentence.

Consider, for example, this passive construction:"The employees were warned by management that compliance with the new e-policy was mandatory and termination would be imposed upon policy violators."

This flabby, passive sentence is 22 words long. You can tighten it up by moving the actors (management and violators) to the beginning of each independent clause, followed by the respective action (warned and termination). Eliminate all unnecessary words and rewrite the sentence as follows: "Management warned employees that compliance with the new e-policy was mandatory and violators would be terminated." Now a trim 16 words, this sentence is easier to read and understand than the original version.

Power Words Vs. Puny Words

There are two types of words in an electronic writer's arsenal. Power words do the work, conveying the meaning of sentences. Puny words act as filler. One of the most effective ways for employees to develop a clean, clear writing style is to eliminate surplus, puny words from sentences.

The electronic writer's goal is to write sentences that contain more power words than puny words. Take these puny sentences for example:"Per the company's proposed e-mail, Internet, and software policies, I want to share my thoughts regarding the effective implementation of the policies and the best way to train employees. I send this to you in the hope of initiating a discussion among all managers."

This forty-four-word construction is unbalanced, with puny words far outweighing power words. Rewritten with the puny words eliminated, the sentence becomes clear and convincing: "Let's schedule a management meeting to discuss the effective implementation of corporate e-policies."

Three Sources of Waste

Compound Constructions

Beware of using multiword phrases, or compound constructions, when one or possibly two words will suffice. Examples of compound constructions include "at that point in time" for "then"; "in the event that" for "if"; and "prior to" rather than "before."

Redundant Pairs

Remember, short and simple are the keys to effective electronic business writing. If you tend to repeat yourself with redundant word pairs like "if and when," "one and only," "each and every," then your electronic writing is probably too fat.

Redundant Modifiers

Do not state the obvious. In the statement "corporate e-mail from headquarters," the word "corporate" is redundant. All e-mail from headquarters would, by its nature, be corporate. Similarly, in "personal use of the company's Internet system is totally banned," the word "totally" is unnecessary, because "banned" says it all.

In addition to adding unnecessary words to what is intended to be brief business correspondence, compound constructions, redundant pairs, and redundant modifiers are trite and overused.

Clear Writing Is Persuasive Writing

A writer's job is to persuade the reader to take action of some sort. The writer may want the e-mail recipient to read the entire message and respond by day's end. Perhaps the organization wants Web site visitors to register to receive a complimentary electronic newsletter. Maybe you would like e-newsletter subscribers to purchase products and services.

Regardless of the goal, persuasion calls for clarity. After all, a reader who cannot decipher the meaning of an e-mail message cannot be expected to take the desired action. Consider the following pointers to help employees produce clear electronic writing:

1. Write in complete words, sentences, and paragraphs, not electronic shorthand. In other words, *don't expct yr rdrs to waste time fgring out what yr msg is about.*

2. Use short, easy-to-read, simple-to-understand words and sentences.

3. Adopt the active voice to energize messages and eliminate unnecessary words.

4. Think about your message from the reader's perspective. Have you provided enough background information and detail to enable your reader to take the desired action?

5. Check for mechanical errors. Spelling, punctuation, and grammatical errors can create confusion and slow the reader down.

Selecting an Appropriate Tone for Electronic Correspondence

Given the immediacy of e-mail, many writers believe it is acceptable to write and send a quick message, without giving much thought to construction or content. Regardless of the nature of the message or the intended reader, it never is acceptable to send an e-mail message that is anything less than its best.

Should a thoughtlessly worded, illogical message land on the screen of "the wrong" reader (the CEO, the company's best customer, a reporter), the results could be disastrous. The writer could suffer a loss of credibility and possible termination. The company risks losing business.

When writing copy for the organization's Web site, e-mail newsletter, or other electronic literature with a long shelf life, employees should adhere to the elements of effective electronic writing.

Consider the Five Ws

Before composing an e-mail message or drafting other electronic copy, instruct employees to focus on the five Ws (who, what, when, where, and why).

Who is your intended reader?

Whether you are drafting an e-mail message to a colleague, writing copy for the organization's Web site, or composing an e-zine for customers and prospects, don't start writing until you have given some thought to your reader's interests, needs, and perspective.

How informed is the reader about your subject? Does the reader have any preconceived notions or prejudices that could influence acceptance of your document? How does the reader view you, your expertise, and your credibility? What will it take to persuade your reader to act?

The answers to these and similar questions will help you structure your message and draft a document that speaks directly to the reader's needs.

What is the main purpose of your e-mail message?

Are you trying to convince readers to act, inform them of a problem, announce an upcoming event, elicit a response to a question? Do you have more than one purpose?

Do not start writing until you have clearly defined your purpose. Once you determine your primary message, repeat, rephrase, and reiterate it throughout your e-mail to ensure the recipient's understanding.

When and where does the action take place?

Is there a deadline the reader should be aware of? Do you need to provide details, such as a meeting time, a street address, or directions?

Before writing, gather every fact the reader will need in order to make a decision. If you omit facts and have to send a follow-up e-mail, you likely will acquire a reputation as a writer who is inattentive to details.

Why should the recipient care about your e-mail message?

How interested in your topic is the reader? Will the reader benefit by acting on your document? Will there be negative fallout if the reader fails to act? What information does the reader need in order to make a decision? Think about your message from the reader's point of view and communicate reader-oriented benefits early in the document.

Take Yourself Out of the Picture

After you have contemplated the five Ws, give some thought to "so what?" As an electronic business writer, your focus should be on your reader, not yourself. Remove your needs, goals, and interests from the writing equation. Place yourself in your reader's screen by asking "so what?" What would it take, in terms of content and composition, to motivate your reader to take the desired action? Once you answer this question, structure a compelling message to drive your e-mail document and capture the intended recipient's attention.

Chapter 14 Recap and E-Action Plan: Creating Accurate, Brief, and Clear E-Copy

1. Focus your e-writing policy on the tenets of accuracy, brevity, and clarity—the ABCs of electronic business writing.

2. As part of your effort to create consistency and clear communication across corporate ranks, make up-to-date dictionaries and

writing style manuals available to employees. If your budget cannot accommodate book purchases, provide employees with a list of approved dictionaries and writing style manuals (see Appendix F for recommendations).

3. Reinforce the concept that speedy does not mean sloppy. Stress the fact that every e-document employees produce reflects upon their professionalism and the organization's credibility.

4. Train e-writers to concentrate on the five Ws (who, what, when, where, and why), and give some thought to "so what?"

5. Bring a professional writing coach on board to introduce employees to your new e-writing policy and provide a refresher on business writing basics and effective electronic writing skills.

Watch Your Cyberlanguage

One of the most effective ways for employers to reduce electronic risks also is one of the simplest. By requiring employees to use appropriate, businesslike language in all electronic communications, employers can limit their liability risks and improve the overall effectiveness of the organization's e-mail and Internet copy in the process.[1]

Controlling Content to Control Risk

Language that is obscene, racist, discriminatory, menacing, harassing, or in any way offensive has no place in the electronic office. Use your e-policy to ban language that could negatively affect your organization's business relationships, damage your corporate reputation, or trigger a lawsuit.

Don't take chances with content. If you have any doubt about your employees' willingness to adhere to a ban on inappropriate language, consider applying a technological solution to your people problem. By installing monitoring software that is programmed to detect and report employee use of "trigger" words, you can stay on top of language violations. As an added bonus, programming your monitoring software to track competitors' names as well as inappropriate language will alert you to any electronic communication that is taking place between your employees and competitors. What you don't know could hurt you. For example, an employee could be planning to open a business or make a career move, using your customer lists, formulas, or trade secrets.

Using Conversational Language

The most effective tone for electronic business correspondence is professional, yet conversational. How do you achieve that tone? Imagine you are at a professional dinner party, attended by colleagues, supervisors, and customers. How would you speak? What type of language would you use? You likely would be conversational, yet professional, using language everyone would understand. Instruct employees to use that same type of language and tone when they write.

Bending a Few Rules to Strike an Appropriate Tone

English is an evolving language, and the rules of good writing are constantly changing. Employees who haven't looked at a writing style manual since their high school or college days may be surprised to learn some of the rules from the "good old days" have relaxed.

Help your employees strike an appropriate conversational business tone by informing them that it is acceptable today to bend the following once-firm rules of grammar:

1. Contractions aren't bad. Unless you're writing a particularly formal document, go ahead and use contractions. We use contractions when we speak in business settings, and there's nothing wrong with incorporating them into your electronic writing.

2. Feel free to end a sentence with a preposition. If you never ended a sentence with a preposition (for, by, at, about, in, to, with, from, etc.), your writing would be extremely stiff, boring, and sometimes unreadable. "What is your e-mail message about?" makes considerably more sense than "About what is your e-mail message?"

3. I, we, and you belong in business writing. The purpose of most e-mail messages is to persuade the reader to take some sort of action. Persuasion requires connection on a human level. It's hard to connect if you depersonalize your writing by eliminating all the pronouns.

4. And another thing. Go right ahead and start your sentence with a coordinating conjunction (and, or, nor, for, but, so, yet) to create a smooth transition from one sentence or thought to another.

Avoiding Sexist Language

In the workplace, sexist language refers not only to harassing and discriminatory comments, jokes, and slurs, it also applies to the overuse of masculine pronouns. With increasing numbers of women in the work force, it is important for electronic writers to avoid sexist language that could offend clients, rankle colleagues, or irritate hidden readers.

In the past, masculine pronouns (he, his, him, etc.) were used to refer both to men and women. No longer is that practice acceptable. Writers now must look for more politically sensitive alternatives. Short of the cumbersome "he/she" and "he or she" construction, what is a gender-sensitive e-writer to do?

Strategies to Keep Electronic Writing Gender-Neutral

1. *Eliminate the offending pronoun.*

Don't Write: The conscientious manager should monitor e-mail that is sent and received by <u>his</u> employees.

Write: The conscientious manager should monitor e-mail that is sent and received by employees.

2. Repeat the noun and rewrite.

Don't Write: The intern could not understand why the chief information officer was so upset when <u>she</u> loaded personal software onto a corporate PC.

Write: The intern could not understand why the chief information officer was so upset when <u>the intern</u> loaded personal software onto a corporate PC.

3. Switch to a plural antecedent noun with a plural pronoun.

Don't Write: <u>An employee</u> should not use the corporate e-mail system to send recipes, jokes, health tips, or other personal messages to <u>his</u> colleagues.

Write: <u>Employees</u> should not use the corporate e-mail system to send recipes, jokes, health tips, or other personal messages to <u>their</u> colleagues.

4. Use the generic pronoun "one."

Don't Write: A business owner is likely to find a written e-policy <u>his</u> best defense against workplace lawsuits.

Write: A business owner is likely to find a written e-policy <u>one's</u> best defense against workplace lawsuits.

5. Rewrite using "who."

Don't Write: The assumption of many employees is that if an e-mail user sends a confidential message to <u>his</u> friend, <u>he</u> can be assured no one else will read it.

Write: The assumption of many employees is that an e-mail user <u>who</u> sends a confidential message to <u>a</u> friend can be assured no one else will read it.

6. Use an article (a, an, the).

Don't Write: The computer security consultant received a performance bonus for <u>his</u> quick response to the company's dastardly hacker attack.

Write: The computer security consultant received a performance bonus for <u>the</u> quick response to the company's dastardly hacker attack.

7. Write in the imperative mood: Issue a command.

Don't Write: No employee is permitted to use <u>his</u> company computer to send or receive harassing, discriminatory, or otherwise offensive e-mail messages.

Write: <u>Employees</u>: Do not use company computers to send or receive harassing, discriminatory, or otherwise offensive e-mail messages.

8. Reword the sentence.

Don't Write: An employee who opts to visit adults-only Internet sites puts <u>his</u> job and <u>his</u> professional reputation at risk.

Write: Visiting adults-only Internet sites will put <u>employees'</u> jobs and professional reputations at risk.

9. Use them, they, or their at the risk of offending some readers.

A long-standing rule of grammar was that a singular antecedent noun takes a singular pronoun. Along with an increased awareness of the importance of a gender-neutral writing style comes a growing acceptance of the use of a plural pronoun (they, them, their) with a singular antecedent noun. While traditionalists discourage the practice, it now is acceptable to write, for example, "<u>An employee</u> who receives a harassing e-mail message should save the message and report the incident to <u>their</u> manager."

Establishing Company-Specific Language Guidelines

General language guidelines prohibiting the use of offensive, sexist, and other types of turnoff language apply to all organizations that are eager to limit content-related e-risks. In addition to these universal language concerns, many companies face special word choice questions and issues that can be addressed effectively as part of the organization's electronic writing policy. Following are points to consider.

1. *Salutations:* Does your organization have a policy that governs the way external readers are addressed? Do you prefer e-mail writers to address customers, clients, and other nonemployees by their titles (Mr., Ms., Dr., Professor, etc.)? Or are first names allowed? If titles are required, at what point in the business relationship—if ever—may employees make the switch to the reader's first name?

    If you have not formally addressed salutations elsewhere, consider doing so in your e-writing policy. This is the type of relatively minor, but potentially thorny, issue that can slow down the writing process for employees who just cannot decide how to address an e-mail recipient.

2. *Signatures:* Have you established rules for message signoff? Giving employees a choice of three standard closes (Sincerely, Cordially, and Best, for example) will speed the writing process and eliminate the possibility of employees' wrapping up business correspondence with quirky signature statements.

3. *Capitalization:* Is there consistency within your organization when it comes to capitalization? How do your employees handle the capitalizing of job titles, departments, job functions, and so forth? Are the words *company* or *firm* to be capitalized every

time they are used? Are all employees clear on what is and what is not to be capitalized? Use your e-writing policy to let employees know what words are to be capitalized and when.

4. **Company name:** Do employees consistently refer to your organization by the same name? If not, is there any chance of creating confusion among readers? Consider adopting a policy whereby, on the first reference, the company name is spelled out in full (XYZ Company, Inc.), then on every subsequent reference, company-approved shorthand may be used (XYZ Company). This type of naming policy prevents employees from using the considerably less formal "XYZ" and saves them the aggravation of writing out the company name in full throughout an e-letter.

5. **Technical terms and professional jargon:** High-tech industries and certain professions (engineering, medicine, and law, for example) tend to have languages of their own. Many industry insiders use technical terms and jargon freely, assuming all readers share their education and experience and will have no trouble understanding the meaning of their words.

   The language of insiders is best restricted to the Intranet and other internal communications. A jargon-laden message that is forwarded to a nontechnical recipient or lands on the screen of a hidden reader could create confusion and lessen the reader's acceptance of future messages from the writer.

6. **Spellings:** Does your organization or industry regularly use words that have optional spellings (theatre/theater, catalogue/catalog, disc/disk, etc.)? Simplify life for your employees by developing a corporate vocabulary list, complete with preferred spellings.

7. **Working around oddities:** In the clicks-and-mortar world, company names sometimes begin with a lowercase letter (e.g., eBay). If that is the case with your company or client companies, address the issue in your employee writing guidelines.

   Since the first word of any sentence must begin with a capital letter, instruct employees to rewrite sentences in which a lowercase company name appears as the first word. Consider the sentence:

> writetobusiness.com, the nation's leading online busi-
> ness writing service, offers executive ghostwriting,
> financial, and business writing services.

This sentence can easily be reworked so that it is grammatically correct:

> The nation's leading online business writing service,
> writetobusiness.com offers executive ghostwriting,
> financial, and business writing services.

Avoid E-Communication Pitfalls

Along with setting company-specific cyberlanguage guidelines, employers would do well to provide employees with a few universal dos and don'ts of electronic communication.

Electronic Humor Is Risky Business

Instruct employees not to incorporate jokes into their electronic business writing. Save the humorous anecdotes for golf outings, luncheon meetings, and other in-person gatherings. Because e-mail is an impersonal medium offering none of the benefits of inflection, facial expression, or body language, electronic humor is risky. Unless written by a professional humorist, electronic jokes are likely to fall flat or be misconstrued by the reader.

At best, an attempt at humor could irritate or agitate the recipient, spelling disaster for a business relationship. Worst case: An employee's "joke" could incite an ugly flame war, a scenario that has no place in the electronic office environment.

Technical Language Can Create E-Confusion

If an employee is sending a technical e-mail to a colleague, customer, supplier, or other reader with shared expertise, it is acceptable to use technical language. But that does not free the writer to draft a dull, unreadable message. Even with technical material, the rules of effective electronic writing hold. Write with the reader in mind, use the active voice, eliminate all unnecessary words, and adhere to the mechanics of good writing by drafting a logical message free of grammar, punctuation, and spelling errors.

What if the intended reader lacks the writer's technical know-how, or if the sender anticipates the message will be forwarded to nontechnical readers? The best advice is to draft the e-mail message itself as a plain-English executive summary of the technical material. More complex technical information then can be provided as an attachment, allowing readers the option of opening it, depending on their interest and technical expertise.

Communicating with International Readers

One of the beauties of e-mail is that it enables writers to communicate quickly and easily with colleagues and customers around the globe. If your employees will be communicating electronically with readers in other countries, be sure to establish communication guidelines and language conventions to simplify the writer's job and enhance reader understanding. Some tips for effective international e-communication are:

1. Remember that international electronic communication poses unique language, cultural, and time challenges. Think about your international reader's communication needs before writing and sending a message abroad.

2. English may be the international language of commerce, but that does not mean every reader, intended and hidden, will have a trouble-free experience with messages written in English. Determine who your reader is and what your reader's needs are before you start writing. If necessary, have your message translated into the language(s) best understood by your intended reader(s).

3. International e-mail calls for more detailed and specific information than domestic e-mail. For example, a message that reads, "The e-policy teleconference will begin at 6 p.m. on 6/5/01," could have disastrous results.

Americans would read that date as June 5, 2001. Europeans would interpret it as May 6, 2001. And the Japanese, using a year, month, day order, would face still more confusion.

Because Europeans use a 24-hour military clock, be sure to write international e-mail according to that format: "The e-policy teleconference will begin at 18:00 on 5 June, 2001."

Similarly, when sending domestic e-mail to business associates in other parts of the United States, be sure to indicate time zone (Eastern Standard Time (EST), Pacific Standard Time (PST), etc.).

Measurements can prove equally challenging when sending e-mail abroad. To eliminate confusion, give the metric measurement, followed by its American equivalent in parentheses. For example, "The staff training facility is located 10 kilometers (6.2 miles) from company headquarters."

4. Do not assume all speakers of a given language are culturally similar. English-speaking Americans differ culturally from the English-speaking populations of Australia, Ireland, and Canada. In fact, some English-speaking Americans differ culturally from other English-speaking Americans who live in other parts of the United States and/or have different ethnic backgrounds. Similarly, Spanish-speaking Mexicans differ culturally from Spaniards, and French-speaking Canadians differ culturally from Parisians.

5. Even when you are sending an e-mail to an employee at one of your organization's own international locations, avoid using technical language, jargon, acronyms, abbreviations, or humor. Given language and cultural differences, there is too much opportunity for misunderstanding and confusion.

6. Be specific and avoid vague language. If you send a hold-the-date message to announce the fact that the company's annual meeting will be held on 25 November, 2001 at a Midwest location, U.S. readers will understand what part of the country you are referring to, but international readers may be in the dark about the Midwest.

Also be mindful of terms that change in meaning depending upon the country in which they are used. In the United States, for example, a boot is a type of shoe. In the United Kingdom, a boot is the trunk of a car. Word choice always plays a significant role in the clarity of communication and the overall effectiveness of e-mail, particularly when international readers are involved.

The Language of Electronic Abbreviations

Electronic writers should use abbreviations to tighten writing only if the reader, intended and hidden, is sure to understand the abbreviations. Instruct employees to use only legitimate and recognizable abbreviations, not their own personal shorthand. Don't overuse abbreviations. Too many abbreviations can make a sentence difficult to read, annoying, and perhaps confusing for the reader. On-screen reading is tough enough without trying to decipher a writer's shorthand, legitimate or not.

When using an uncommon abbreviation, be sure to clarify it on the first reference by spelling out the word or phrase and citing the abbreviation in parentheses. The abbreviation may then be used alone throughout the rest of the document. For example, "The Software and Information Industry Association (SIIA) is the principal trade association of the PC software industry."

Electronic Abbreviations Create New Challenges

With e-communication spawning a vocabulary of its own, electronic abbreviations have found their way into e-mail messages and Internet chat. Some electronic abbreviations (FYI and FAQ, for example) would be familiar to nearly all readers. Other e-abbreviations rarely are used, however, and are unlikely to be recognized by the majority of electronic business writers.

As with traditional abbreviations, electronic ones should be avoided if there is any doubt the intended reader will understand their meaning. Remember, the electronic writer's job is to communicate clearly with readers, not to show off knowledge of the "secret" language of cyberspace. Some popular electronic abbreviations are:

BCNU	be seeing you
BRB	be right back
BTW	by the way
CUL	see you later
F2F	face to face
FAQ	frequently asked question
FOAF	friend of a friend
FWIW	for what it's worth
FYA	for your amusement
FYEO	for your eyes only
FYI	for your information
GMTA	great minds think alike
HHOK	ha-ha, only kidding
IMHO	in my humble opinion
IOW	in other words
LOL	laughing out loud
MOTOS	member of the opposite sex
MOTSS	member of the same sex
MSGS	messages
NLT	no later than
OBTW	oh, by the way
OIC	oh, I see
PLS	please
PMFJI	pardon me for jumping in
PRES	presentation
PTP	pardon the pun

QTY'S	quantities
REC'D	received
RGDS	regards
ROTF	rolling on the floor
ROTFL	rolling on the floor laughing
THX	thanks
TIA	thanks in advance
TMRW	tomorrow
TTFN	ta-ta for now
WB	welcome back
WRT	with regards to
WTG	way to go
YR	your

Smileys Can Warm Up or Dumb Down Communication

Unlike one-on-one meetings and telephone conversations, e-mail is a communications tool that is totally devoid of inflection, facial expression, and body language. To help readers interpret the e-writer's attitude and tone, "smileys" (also known as emoticons) have been created as visual shorthand. Created with standard keyboard characters, smileys are used by some electronic writers to substitute for facial expression and body language. The smiley generally follows the punctuation mark at the end of the sentence.

The equivalent of e-mail slang, smileys have no place in business writing. Readers who are unfamiliar with smileys won't understand their meaning. Readers who do understand smileys likely will interpret their use as a sign that the writer is not being professional. Employees should rely on the strength of their writing, rather than smileys, exclamation points, and uppercase letters, to communicate electronic messages effectively.

Common E-Mail Smileys

:-)	happy, smiling, kidding, grinning
:-[	sad sarcasm
:-(	sad, angry, chagrined
;-(	feel like crying
:-&	tongue-tied
:!-(	crying
:-<	very upset
%-)	eyes crossed, smirking
:-II	angry
:-(o)	yelling
:-*	kiss
:-D	laughing, demonic laugh
:-\	undecided
;-)	winking
:-#	my lips are sealed
>:P	sticking tongue out
:-P	sticking tongue out
8-)	wide eyed
8-O	shocked, amazed
:-I	apathetic
:-/	skeptical, perplexed, resigned
:-o	amazed, shocked
:->	sarcastic smile
:-]	smirk, happy sarcasm
<:/&	stomach in knots
>:)	devilish
O:-)	angelic
X-(	brain dead

In addition to smileys, some electronic writers use a form of electronic shorthand—a combination of smileys and abbreviations—to indicate emotion and warm up e-mail. As with smileys and abbreviations, electronic shorthand has almost no place in business writing. Shorthand should be used only in informal correspondence, and never should be used if there is any chance the reader will be confused. Examples of common e-shorthand include:

Shorthand Symbol	Emotion Indicated
<g>	grin
<grin>	grin
<s>	sigh
<gasp>	gasp
<l>	laugh
<lol>	laughing out loud
<jk>	just kidding
<>	no comment

Chapter 15 Recap and E-Action Plan: Controlling Content to Control Risk

1. Address cyberlanguage issues in your e-writing policy. One of the easiest, most effective ways to control risk is by controlling content. Train your employees to monitor their electronic language, adopting a conversational tone appropriate for business communications.

2. Help your employees strike an appropriate, conversational business tone by offering an e-business writing refresher course.

3. Instruct employees to avoid sexist language and turnoff words. Jokes, technical language, and jargon should be avoided too.

4. Establish guidelines for effective international e-communication.

5. Electronic abbreviations, smileys, and e-shorthand have no place in business communication.

Formatting Written E-Policies, E-Mail Messages, and Internet Copy

In formatting your organization's written e-mail, Internet, and software usage policies, the goals are readability and accessibility. You want to create policy documents that are easy for employees and managers to read, understand, and act upon. Tips to enhance the readability of your written e-policies follow.

Keep Policies Brief

Don't produce one long e-policy document that covers e-mail, Internet, and software usage and expect employees to read it. Chances are, they won't. Increase the odds of having your e-policies read, remembered, and adhered to by writing and distributing three separate and slim policy documents. Keep each policy short, simple, and straight to the point.

Incorporate White Space into Policies

Use white space, or blank space, to enhance readability and add visual impact to your policies. While the use of white space will result in longer documents, the tradeoff is worth it. A ten-page, double-spaced document that is accessible and easy to read is considerably less intimidating than a two-page, single-spaced policy that is crammed full, margin to margin and header to footer, with nonstop information written in a tight, tiny typeface.

To maximize white space and enhance visual appeal:

- Double-space your document.

- Leave margins of at least an inch on both sides. Learning goes up when notes are written, so consider leaving even more space and encouraging employees to use the margins for notes. Make it easy for employees to jot down important lessons as they work through training.

- Incorporate an extra line or two before and after an important section to make the copy stand out.

Rely on Bold Headlines and Subheads in Policies

Emphasize important copy points while using as few words as possible. Headlines and subheads can help employees navigate through the e-policy document. Stick with standard typefaces. Use a larger font, perhaps 14 point, and bold type to make headlines and subheads stand out.

Include a Table of Contents in Each Policy

Make it easy for employees to locate information quickly as questions arise and concerns develop.

E-Mail and Internet Formatting Guidelines

As part of your comprehensive e-policy, you will want to establish formatting guidelines to help your employees make the most of their e-mail messages and Internet copy. If e-mail is dense, the recipient may not have the patience to work through it. When it comes to formatting e-mail, readability is the writer's primary concern. Guidelines for making e-mail as readable as possible follow.[1]

Select the Right Typeface

E-mail that is composed of unusual type or exceptionally large or small characters is just plain hard to read. Electronic business correspondence calls for a polished, professional look. Accomplish that by using a standard typeface, such as Times New Roman, Courier, or Arial. Enhance reader comfort by sticking with 10-point, 11-point, or 12-point font sizes. A good typeface policy for business e-mail is not too small, not too large, not too fancy.

Resist the Urge to Use Capital or Lowercase Letters

In an effort to draw attention to on-screen messages, many e-mail correspondents write entirely in the uppercase. But a message written in all uppercase letters is more difficult to read than one composed in standard style.

The human eye is used to reading a mix of uppercase and lowercase letters. When you draft e-mail entirely in the uppercase, you risk slowing down and possibly annoying a reader who is unaccustomed to this type of visual presentation. By the same token, resist the urge to write e-mail messages entirely in the lowercase. It may be quicker to write in all uppercase or lowercase letters, but the result will be a document that is difficult to read.

Create Visual Emphasis

You will save writing time and ease the reader's job as well by emphasizing important points with lists of numbers or bullet substitutes. Because there is no standard bullet character on the keyboard, you can insert an asterisk (*) or a dash (-) instead. Suggest that your employees adhere to these tips for adding electronic emphasis:

- Be consistent. Lists that start with an asterisk should end with an asterisk.

▓ Adopt one style and stick with it. Write lists either as complete sentences or sentence fragments. Just be consistent.

▓ Begin each new bullet point with a capital letter.

Numbered lists create the greatest emphasis. Maximize impact by:

1. Keeping copy brief and lines short.

2. Indenting lists.

3. Double-spacing lists and leaving plenty of white space.

As an alternative to numbered lists, you can construct lists within paragraphs. This approach saves space while maximizing readability. Example: "E-policies are implemented most successfully when management adheres to three training principles: (1) inform employees of the e-risks faced by the company as a whole and employees individually; (2) create continuing education tools to reinforce training; and (3) enforce policies and penalties consistently."

Limit Most E-Mail to One Screen Page

Usually, an e-mail message should be contained on one screen, and only a small portion of the screen at that. On occasion, however, you may need to write an e-mail message that is so long the reader must scroll the screen in order to read the entire message. That is not necessarily bad. Some topics warrant a little extra space. If, for example, you publish an e-mail newsletter, your document may well exceed one screen page.

When you start to think your e-mail message has gone on too long, or if you need to support your message with letterhead, charts, graphics, or written backup, then it is time to consider attaching a separate document to your message. Do not attach and send a file, however, without first referring to the attachment policies of the sender's and receiver's organization (see Chapter 8).

Mind Your Mechanical Matters

Write in complete words and grammatically correct sentences. Proofread and spell-check your message before you hit "send."

Emphasize Electronic Text

Because of incompatibility problems among software packages, many electronic writers have adopted certain conventions for italicizing and underlining electronic text. Incorporate these electronic symbols into your organization's e-writing policy to ensure consistency and eliminate confusion.

To Italicize Type

Insert an asterisk (*) on either side of the word or phrase to be italicized. For example, to italicize the word "private," surround it with asterisks: "The marketing director ignored corporate e-policy and sent her fiancé a *private* e-love note on Valentine's Day." In this case, "private" is italicized to indicate that in reality, a "private" e-mail message is anything but private. The marketing director's e-love note could well have been monitored by management or read by her fiancé's group list, if he accidentally forwarded it.

To Underline Type

Add the underscore (_) character before and after the copy to be underlined. For example, to underline *The Chicago Manual of Style,* introduce and follow the book title with an underscore character: "The organization's e-writing policy states that employees are to refer to_The Chicago Manual of Style_for questions of usage and style."

Chapter 16 Recap and E-Action Plan: Establishing E-Formatting Guidelines

1. Increase the effectiveness of e-policies by decreasing the length of documents. Keep e-policies short, simple, and straight to the point.

2. Use white space to enhance readability.

3. Provide navigational tools (headlines, subheads, bold type, large fonts) to help employees read and understand your e-policies.

4. Establish formatting guidelines to help employees create effective e-mail messages and Internet copy that is easily read and acted upon.

PART **five**

Getting Employees

On-Board with Your

Online Policy

Rallying the Support of Managers

You can devote enormous amounts of time and talent to researching, planning, and writing your organization's e-policies, only to see them fail if you don't devote an equal amount of attention to policy implementation. You cannot expect your e-policies to succeed without a thorough, ongoing commitment to employee education. Effective e-policy education begins with your managers and supervisors. Before communicating new e-policies to employees, you must get managers on board as policy advocates and enforcers. It is essential that you conduct management training prior to employee training. Give your management team ample time to ask questions and express concerns they may not be comfortable communicating in front of employees. Do not proceed with employee training until you are certain all managers are 100 percent behind the organization's e-risk management goals and are committed to enforcing your e-mail, Internet, and software usage policies.

If you sense resistance among some managers, spend a little extra time discussing their concerns. Workplace e-risk and e-policy are relatively new concepts. Do not expect all managers and employees to understand or appreciate the dangers inherent in e-communication and e-commerce. For best results, make e-policy training an ongoing educational program, not a one-time session.

In the Battle against E-Risks, Managers Form the Front Line of Defense

The success of your e-policy program depends on management's willingness to embrace the organization's e-mail, Internet, and software usage policies, and then rally the troops' support for the policies. Your training goals for managers differ from employee training goals. Not only do you want managers and supervisors to comply with the e-policies themselves, you also want them to enforce the policies within their departments.

Educate managers about the risks inherent in, and the costs associated with, inappropriate e-mail, Internet, and software use. Managers who are responsible for departmental hiring, training, and budgeting will understand the financial loss and productivity drain e-risks represent.

You may want to support management education by developing a special e-leadership training manual. Include a recap of your organization's e-risks, an executive summary of the employee audit you conducted at the beginning of the e-policy process, netiquette guidelines for managers (see Chapter 9), and an overview of the disciplinary action employees will face if they fail to comply with the organization's e-policies.

Train Your Trainers

Once your organization's e-policies are introduced to employees, rely on your managers, along with your human resources and information management departments, to conduct ongoing employee training and enforce e-policy compliance. Following are a few training tips to share with managers who may or may not be experienced trainers.

1. *Understand that most employees are concerned about themselves first, the organization second.* When training employees, focus less on organizational e-risks and more on the penalties employees will face for noncompliance. Employees will look to their managers for clear direction on what they need to

do, and what they should avoid doing, in order to comply with e-policies, avoid disciplinary action, and hold onto their jobs.

2. *Treat employees fairly and with professional respect.* Assure them that they will not be disciplined for computer system abuses that occurred prior to the development of the company's e-policies. Make it clear, however, that with the company's e-policies now in place, employees will face disciplinary action—possibly termination—for policy violations.

3. *Enforce the organization's e-mail, Internet, and software usage policies consistently.* You do not want to develop a reputation for going easy on some violators, while throwing the book at others. A manager's failure to enforce e-policies consistently and in accordance with organizational guidelines should result in disciplinary action against, and possible termination of, the manager.

4. *Do not turn your back on software piracy.* And don't fool yourself into believing you are saving the organization money (thus doing a good job) by overlooking or encouraging illegal software duplication.

If a disgruntled employee or vengeful former employee were to report a manager's illegal actions to the Software & Information Industry Association, the company could face a lengthy period of business interruption, lost productivity, six-figure fines, public embarrassment, and negative publicity. Managers who condone software piracy will suffer the same penalties as employees who copy software illegally.

Managers' Tip Sheet: Answers to Employees' Most Common E-Policy Questions

To smooth the effective introduction of your e-mail, Internet, and software usage policies, provide managers with a list of the questions and concerns employees are most likely to have.

Use employee responses to the E-Mail, Internet, and Software Usage Questionnaire (see Chapter 2) to structure your customized

Managers' Tip Sheet. Along with issues of specific concern to your employees, incorporate the following general questions and answers.

Q. Isn't it illegal for my employer to read my e-mail?

A. No, it is not illegal. In fact, according to the federal Electronic Communications Privacy Act (ECPA), an employer-provided computer system is the property of the employer. As such, the company has the right to monitor all e-mail traffic and Internet surfing that occurs on the company's system.

Q. What happens if a co-worker sends me an obscene or offensive e-mail message? Am I going to lose my job because of someone else's action?

A. You cannot control other employees' actions, but you can control your own. If you receive an offensive e-mail message from another employee, take the following steps: (1) Do not forward, delete, or reply to the message. Leave it in your electronic mailbox for management review. (2) Report the incident to the human resources director. Management will handle the situation from there. (3) Do not fall prey to temptation. Even though other employees may be violating e-mail policy, it is important for you to adhere to it as well as the organization's Internet and software usage policies.

Q. I use e-mail to stay in touch with my kids during the day. They check in with me after school via e-mail, and they know to use e-mail in an emergency if they cannot reach me by phone. Do I have to tell my children to stop e-mailing me?

A. No. Management recognizes that some personal e-mail use is warranted. While the e-policy clearly states that the company's e-mail system is reserved for business use, the policy certainly allows for brief communication between work and home. And, of course, e-mail may be used to communicate in the case of personal emergencies.

The type of personal communication that is prohibited includes any correspondence that pulls you away from your job for extended periods of time. Also prohibited are the posting of personal messages, such as advertising a garage sale, soliciting a charitable donation, or campaigning for a political candidate. And, most significantly, you are prohibited from sending any message, personal or business-related, that is in any way offensive, menacing, or discriminatory.

If you are confused about what constitutes appropriate and acceptable e-mail use, please talk with your immediate supervisor or see the HR manager or chief information officer.

Q. Why can't I bring my own software from home into the office? If I paid for it and it will help me do my job, what's the problem?

A. When you purchase software, you don't actually buy the software itself. You purchase a license to load the software onto one computer. It is illegal to load software that has a single-user license onto multiple computers. The term for this is *soft-loading*.

In addition to being ethically wrong, softloading puts the company at risk on a number of levels. You could carry a virus into the office via your software. If illegally duplicated software malfunctions, you will not be able to access technical support through the manufacturer's helpline. And, if the software police come calling and find illegal software on your workstation computer (or any other employees' computers), it is the company, not the individual employee, who will be held liable.

Q. I know of two supervisors who are visiting adults-only Internet sites. I've seen pornographic images on their computer screens as I've passed by their offices. What should I do? I know they are violating the company's Internet policy, but I'm afraid I'll lose my job if I turn them in.

A. The organization's e-mail, Internet, and software usage policies apply to all employees, managers and supervisors as well as staff. If you know of any employee who is violating company e-policy, please alert the human resources director. The information you provide will be held in strict confidence and will be checked out thoroughly. If a violation is unearthed, appropriate action will be taken.

Remember, though, confidentiality is your responsibility, too. You can count on the human resources director to keep your name out of the investigation. Your involvement will not remain secret, however, if you choose to discuss the situation with other employees.

Q. Will I lose my job if a malicious hacker attacks the company's network and shuts us down for a long period of time?

A. The company has taken precautions to avoid the type of denial of service attack that would shut it down for an extended period. It has conducted an internal e-risk assessment and put into place an e-risk management policy, assessed and shored up computer security capabilities and procedures, developed comprehensive e-mail, Internet, and software policies, and devoted time and energy to employee education.

There is no way to predict when or how e-disaster may strike, or what impact an electronic crisis would have on the company and its employees. However, if all employees do their best to comply with the organization's written e-policies, then the likelihood of an e-disaster occurring is greatly reduced.

Q. I've heard the term *social engineering* associated with hackers, but I'm unclear what it means or how it applies to me. Please explain.

A. When hackers prey on the naiveté of employees or the carelessness of employers in order to gain information about and access to a computer system, that is called social engineering.

Don't make it easy for hackers to access the company's computer system. Follow the procedures outlined in the corporate e-mail and Internet policies. Do not share your password with anyone. Do not post or keep lists of passwords in unsecured locations. Turn off your computer if you are going to be away from your desk for more than an hour. Unless you specifically have been authorized to do so, do not divulge information about the company's computer system to any outsider, in person, on the phone, or via e-mail.

Q. No one expects e-mail messages to be well-written and error-free. With e-mail, a typo is just a typo. No big deal! So why should I adhere to the rules spelled out in the company's e-writing policy?

A. Every message you write, whether electronic or on paper, is a reflection of the company's credibility and your professionalism. Your e-mail correspondence is expected to be just as polished and professional as your written letters and proposals. Check every e-mail message for accuracy, brevity, and clarity. Run each document through spell check. And adhere to the writing guidelines outlined in the company's e-writing manual. If you need a business-writing refresher, bring this to the attention of your supervisor or the company training manager.

Chapter 17 Recap and E-Action Plan: Managers Hold the Key to E-Policy Success

1. Effective e-policy education begins with your managers and supervisors. Before communicating your new e-policies to employees, get managers on board as e-policy advocates and enforcers.

2. Educate managers about the risks and costs of inappropriate e-mail, Internet, and software use.

3. Develop training tools for managers. Create an e-leadership training manual that recaps e-risks, summarizes employee audit findings, reviews netiquette guidelines, answers employees' most common questions, and provides a breakdown, by violation, of the disciplinary action employees will face if they fail to comply with the organization's e-policies.

18

Instilling a Sense of E-Policy Ownership among Employees

To be successful, your organization's e-mail, Internet, and software usage policies must be embraced by your employees. It is not enough to draft a policy, review it once with employees, and then store it on a shelf in the HR director's office. That type of passive approach suggests that management is not really serious about the policies and gives people little reason to comply with them.

Effective e-risk management depends, in part, on your success at creating in workers and managers a sense of e-policy ownership. Employees who view the company's e-policies as "their" documents, created with their input, career development, and job safety in mind, are more likely to support policy enforcement.

If you conducted the employee E-Mail, Internet, and Software Usage Questionnaire outlined in Chapter 2, you already have taken the first step toward establishing a sense of employee ownership. If the audit was conducted appropriately, in a confidential and non-threatening way, many employees already may view the policies as "their" documents. They will appreciate the fact that rather than creating policies in a vacuum and imposing them on the staff, management incorporated employee comments and feedback.

Other employees, not yet recognizing the valuable role they played in shaping the organization's e-policies, may not share their co-workers' appreciation for the documents. For these employees, training will play a particularly valuable role.

Tips for Training Employees

Because of the newness of e-risks and e-policies, the most effective way to notify employees of your e-policies is in person. Depending on the size of your organization, you may want to hold a single group meeting for all employees. Larger organizations may choose a series of smaller meetings, held over a period of one or two days. Training tips to help rally employee support and compliance follow:

1. Show employees you mean business by having a senior company official (the more senior the better) introduce the organization's e-policies.

2. If the senior executive wants to conduct the entire training program, that's great. Otherwise, assign in-house experts from various departments the role of e-policy trainers. Your human resources director, chief information officer, cyberlawyer, and public relations director could each be called on to review various aspects of the e-policies with employees.

3. Begin training with a recap of the employee e-questionnaire and e-risks uncovered by the audit. Employees will appreciate the fact that you are keeping them in the loop. Your e-mail, Internet, and software usage policies will have more meaning if employees believe they played a role in policy development. On a more personal note, most employees will appreciate knowing where they stand in comparison to other employees' computer use, misuse, and abuse.

4. Distribute printed copies of the organization's e-mail, Internet, and software usage policies. Walk employees through each policy, point by point. Encourage questions and discussion. Having e-policy team experts on hand to answer questions and address concerns will help reduce resistance and increase the likelihood of compliance.

5. Do not wrap up training until you are certain all employees understand each e-policy and what constitutes appropriate—and inappropriate—use of the organization's computer assets.

6. If your policies include e-mail and Internet monitoring, say so.

7. Explain to employees exactly what type of personal use is acceptable, and what is unacceptable.

8. Review penalties thoroughly. Make it clear that policy violations will result in disciplinary action or termination.

9. Ask every employee to sign and date two copies of each e-policy, acknowledging the employee has read and understands it.

10. Provide each employee with a signed copy of each policy. Place a master set of the written policies in the organization's employee handbook. Make electronic copies of the e-policies accessible through the company's Intranet system.

Continuing Education Is Directly Linked to Success

To ensure e-policy compliance and success, integrate a program of continuing education. Develop ongoing methods to reinforce training among managers and employees. Send policy reminders via e-mail. Hold periodic training sessions to update employees on policy changes. Make annual e-policy training mandatory for all employees and managers. Post policy updates on the company's Intranet site. Put e-policy reminders in paycheck envelopes.

In short, do what it takes to raise employees' e-consciousness and keep them focused on the role employees play in making the company's e-risk management initiative a success.

Don't Forget to Train Your E-Writers and E-Crisis Response Team

In addition to educating employees about the ins and outs of the organization's e-mail, Internet, and software policies, you may want to develop additional training programs to enhance employees' electronic writing (see Part 4) and crisis communications skills (see Part 6).

Chapter 18 Recap and E-Action Plan: Training, Training, and More Training

1. Make it easy for employees to access e-policy information. Provide each employee with a signed copy of the policies and keep master copies of the e-mail, Internet, and software policies in your comprehensive employee handbook.

2. Make employees fully aware of the penalties—including possible termination—associated with e-policy violations.

3. Successful employee training is not a one-time event. Create continuing education programs and tools to reinforce training and ensure e-policy compliance.

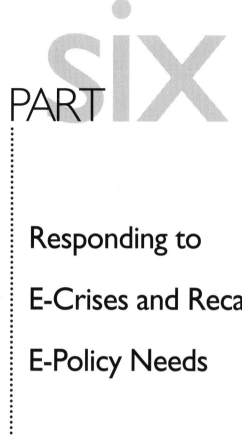

PART SIX

Responding to

E-Crises and Recapping

E-Policy Needs

Fighting Internet Disaster
Drafting an E-Crisis Communications Policy

Hoping for the Best, Preparing for the Worst

By all accounts, you have done everything right. You have conducted a thorough internal audit to determine how employees are using your company's computer assets and to assess the specific e-risks facing your organization. With the help of legal counsel, you have drafted comprehensive e-mail, Internet, and software usage policies for review and sign-off by full- and part-time employees, independent contractors, and temporary staff. You have conducted training for managers and staff to ensure that everyone understands why the organization has implemented e-policies and what is expected of each employee. You have established a program of monitoring employees' e-mail and Internet use. You have retained computer security consultants and e-insurance experts to shore up security problems, minimize e-exposures, and help reduce the likelihood of litigation and other costly problems. And you have provided employees with electronic writing and cyberlanguage guidelines in an effort to reduce risks by controlling content.

If you are lucky, your employees will adhere to your e-policies, your managers will enforce the e-policies effectively, and your organization will enjoy a trouble-free journey through cyberspace. Employers who are not so lucky, however, may find themselves embroiled in the type of high-profile crisis situations that can wreck business reputations and sink corporate revenues if not handled properly.

Are You Prepared to Handle an E-Crisis?

Would you know what to do if you landed on the wrong side of a sexual harassment lawsuit stemming from offensive e-mail correspondence among employees? Could you deftly handle phone calls from reporters baiting you with questions about why you have created a work environment that is openly hostile to women?

How would you respond if a television reporter stuck a live microphone in your face and asked about your practice of hiring sexual predators? Could you maintain composure while a television news crew filmed your business partner being led away in handcuffs, charged with e-mailing pornography to children?

What would you do if, following a hacker attack and system collapse, your telephone system were deluged with calls from angry customers and pushy reporters who, facing deadlines, were prepared to file stories with or without your input?

Would you be prepared to deal with business interruption, public embarrassment, six-figure fines, and negative publicity if federal agents appeared at your door in response to an informant's tip that your computers were loaded with stolen software?

More importantly, how would your employees—from senior managers to entry-level staff—react if faced with an e-crisis?

The Potential for Electronic Crises Is Huge

Well-written, effectively communicated e-mail, Internet, and software usage policies can go a long way toward preventing an e-crisis. But even the best policies and most thorough employee-training program cannot guarantee absolute protection.

The qualities—speed, convenience, and ease of operation—that make e-mail such an appealing way to communicate also make it dangerous. People often treat e-mail recklessly, writing comments they would never dream of saying out loud. An employee who would not tell an ethnic joke, spread a nasty rumor about the boss, or bad-mouth a colleague in person sometimes will feel free to do so via e-mail.

Many e-mail users take false comfort in the belief that their messages will be read only by their intended readers. The erroneous assumption that e-mail messages can be deleted easily and permanently with the simple stroke of a key can add to the electronic writer's false sense of security.

People Problems Cannot Be Avoided

No matter how in-depth your preemployment interviews and psychological testing procedures may be, a problem employee occasionally will slip through the system. And even the best employees now and then may be tempted to misuse corporate computer resources.

Unless Internet monitoring software detects it, you may never know that a trusted employee has a gambling addiction and spends the majority of the workday visiting online casinos. Until the police show up at your door with an arrest warrant, you may be ignorant of the fact that a senior manager has been using the company computer system to solicit sex from underage girls. Unless a competitor rolls out a product identical to the one your organization has spent thousands of hours and millions of dollars developing, you may never know a once-trusted employee downloaded proprietary information prior to jumping ship.

If Internet industry giants like Yahoo!, eBay, and Amazon.com can be hacked, if heavily protected institutions like the Air Force and Navy can be cracked, if high-security installations like the Pentagon can be infiltrated 250,000 times a year,[1] how can your organization hope to be completely safe from predatory cyberattacks? While computer security, e-policies, and e-insurance can help reduce the likelihood of attacks and the costs associated with them, there are no

guarantees in cyberspace. And there is no end to the panic and dis-
ruption a malicious hacker, cyberextortionist, or an otherwise good
employee engaged in rash online behavior can cause.

Incorporate Crisis Communications Planning into E-Policy Development

Hope for the best, but prepare for the worst. If yours is a large company with deep pockets, you may want to purchase a crisis communications insurance policy (see Chapter 6) as an added layer of protection against e-disaster. Crisis communications insurance will
enable you to retain an experienced (and expensive) media relations
firm or crisis communications consultant to deal with the media and
the public on your behalf should e-disaster strike.

For smaller organizations with budgets that do not accommodate the purchase of crisis communications insurance, planning is key.
Act now, when there is no disaster in sight, to develop a written e-
crisis communications policy. Prepare your organization today to
implement your plan immediately in the event of a crisis tomorrow.
When it comes to developing a workable e-crisis communications
policy and dealing with the media and the public during a disaster,
consider these basic rules.

1. Make your e-crisis communications policy a blueprint for action.
   Incorporate the plan into your organization's overall e-policy.
   Review it with all employees to ensure that everyone knows
   who is responsible for what in the event of a crisis. A good crisis
   communications policy should provide complete details about
   what each employee is to do, and not do, following a crisis. The
   plan also should provide instructions for post-crisis follow-up.

2. Consider your audiences. The media represent your primary
   communications concern during a crisis. But don't forget to communicate with other important audiences who have a stake in
   your organization and the outcome of your crisis. Keep employees fully informed to help alleviate fears about the safety of their
   jobs and the stability of your organization. If your company is

public, you should be prepared to answer tough questions from worried shareholders and what may be a shaken investment community.

3. Address customer complaints and questions promptly and fully throughout the crisis. As part of your e-crisis communications policy, consider developing a special customer service program for implementation immediately following an e-disaster. Implement a post-crisis customer service program to thank the customers who stuck by you during the crisis and win back customers who took their business elsewhere as a result of your e-disaster.

4. Yes, this is the age of electronic communication, but that includes the telephone as well as the computer. If you don't have a toll-free 800 phone number, get one. And be sure to cite the number on all electronic documents and printed materials. If your computer system goes down and triggers a crisis, you want to make it easy for employees, customers, the media, shareholders, and others to reach you by phone.

5. Establish a crisis management leadership team. Involve your in-house lawyer or outside legal counsel, the organization's chief information officer, your public relations/media relations director or consultant, and a senior company official—the more senior the better. Assign these professionals the task of overseeing development of your written e-crisis communications policy. Make the e-crisis team responsible for assigning emergency response roles to staff and implementing the written policy in a timely and effective manner should electronic disaster strike.

6. Establish an emergency response team. Assign specific crisis communications tasks to managers and employees who are reachable and can be relied on to get the job done. List all team members' home, cellular, and car phone numbers in your crisis communications document. As emergency response team members resign or retire, appoint replacements immediately. Assign trained standbys to fill in for ill or vacationing emergency response team mem-

bers. A cybercrisis could occur at any moment. Do not allow emergency response team positions to go unfilled.

7. Assign one senior spokesperson to respond to all media inquiries. Make sure all employees know that in a crisis situation, only the assigned e-crisis spokesperson is authorized to speak with reporters. Caution employees against taking reporters' calls at home or acquiescing to media ambushes in the company parking lot. Comments from multiple spokespersons, particularly unauthorized and ill-informed persons, can lead to contradictions and confusion that could cost the organization its credibility.

8. Enroll your e-crisis spokesperson in professional media training if your spokesperson is uncomfortable answering reporters' tough questions or ill at ease on camera. A spokesperson who falters when answering questions, looks nervous, or responds angrily to questions will not do your already injured organization any good.

9. Be prepared. Use crisis communications planning as an opportunity to anticipate e-crisis scenarios and likely questions from the media, customers, and others. Preparation will enable you to control interviews by stressing the points you want to make, rather than merely responding to the questions asked.

10. After you prepare your e-crisis communications policy, don't just stick it on a shelf and forget about it. Review the policy with managers and staff as part of organizationwide training to ensure that employees know who is to do what, when, in the event of an e-crisis. Following the initial policy introduction, conduct annual training as a refresher for long-term employees and an introduction for new hires.

Avoid Common Media Relations Mistakes

When experiencing a cybercrisis, avoid making common media relations mistakes.

Do Not Hide from the Media

If a crisis hits, greet it head on. You may not like it, but the media come along for the ride during any high-profile crisis. Rather than trying to hide from reporters, work with them. You don't have to tell journalists everything you know, but you should never stonewall them. Give the media as much honest information as you can, then stop talking.

"Never pick a fight with anyone who buys ink by the barrel" is the adage media relations professionals live by. Hide from a reporter on deadline or lie to a journalist who is just trying to do a job and you may find your company the subject of not just one, but several negative stories.

Never Go "Off the Record" with a Reporter

Nothing you say to the press is really "off the record." Once the words are out of your mouth, you cannot take them back. Confusion reigns in crisis situations, and it is easy for reporters to confuse on-the-record comments with those that are intended to remain confidential. In almost all situations, the best advice is to say what you would feel comfortable reading the next morning in your local newspaper, then stop talking.

If, for some reason, you feel your organization would be best served by providing a reporter with off-the-record background information or confidential material of some sort, then take time to structure a formal off-the-record arrangement with the reporter. That involves meeting, in person or on the phone, with both the reporter and the reporter's editor. State your terms, and do not proceed until both the reporter and editor agree to handle the situation as you request.

What type of off-the-record terms could you negotiate? You might offer to provide deep background information with the stipulation that neither your name nor the organization's name be associated with the tip. Or you could offer a statement for attribution (provide a quote) if you are identified only as an "employee of the company," without your title, department, rank (senior, entry-level), or sex given.

When negotiating off-the-record arrangements, it is important to bear in mind how easy it is for readers and viewers to figure out who a reporter's secret source is. In off-the-record situations, you are responsible for protecting your own anonymity. You cannot rely on the reporter to do that job for you. That is why the best advice is to avoid off-the-record situations entirely.

Never Lie to the Press

You don't have to tell the media everything you know, but never say anything that is not true. If asked a question you cannot answer, respond by saying something that casts your organization in a good light, while giving the media something they may be able to incorporate into a story.

For example, if asked how vicious hackers were able to crack your system, you could formulate a response like the following. "It's too early in our investigation to know exactly how the hackers were able to penetrate our system. But as you know, malicious hacking has become a major problem in the United States and around the world. Our organization remains committed to working with the federal government and the computer industry to put a stop to this problem once and for all."

Do Not Lose Control of the Interview

Never repeat loaded questions, speculate, or allow a reporter to put words in your mouth. If, for instance, a reporter were to ask, "What made your company so vulnerable to a malicious hacker attack?" don't repeat the reporter's verbiage or in any way acknowledge your vulnerability.

Instead, take control of the interview by focusing on the story you want to tell. Share information about the high-tech security procedures and written policies you have put in place to minimize electronic risks.

Never Say "No Comment"

Many people take "no comment" as an admission of guilt. If you cannot respond to a question, explain why you cannot comment, then offer whatever alternative information you feel comfortable sharing. Were a reporter to ask how long a period of business interruption you anticipate following a hacker attack, you might sidestep the question of time and give a response like, "We have experienced technology and security experts working around the clock to resolve this unfortunate situation."

Avoid Giving "Yes" and "No" Answers

You will look as though you have something to hide if that is all you say. Be concise. Be quotable. Take control of each interview situation. View every post-crisis interview as an opportunity to tell your story to customers, shareholders, employees, the media, and other important audiences.

Chapter 19 Recap and E-Action Plan: Managing E-Disaster Effectively

1. Do not allow an electronic crisis to catch you off guard. Incorporate an e-crisis communications policy into your overall e-policy.

2. Don't stop with a written policy. Your cybercrisis policy is only as good as your ability to communicate and implement it. Assign trusted professionals to draft the e-crisis plan. Establish a crisis response team to manage the damage should the worst happen.

3. Conduct training that includes media skills training for your spokesperson, if necessary, as well as implementation training for your crisis response team.

4. Keep your e-crisis plan current with an annual review and training program. Update the names and phone numbers of your crisis management leadership team, corporate spokesperson, and emergency response team on an annual basis, at least.

5. In the event of an electronic disaster, remember that you, not the media, are in control. Refer to your written e-crisis communica-

tions policy. Adhere to the rules of effective crisis communications. Avoid common media relations blunders. Focus on overcoming your e-disaster and getting your operation back on track as efficiently and cost-effectively as possible.

20

E-Policy Dos and Don'ts

DO

1. Establish comprehensive, written e-policies that address employee use of e-mail, the Internet, and software.

2. Educate employees about software piracy. Ensure compliance with all software licenses.

3. Communicate the fact that the organization's e-mail and Internet systems are to be used strictly as business communications tools. But don't stop there. Provide clear guidance on what is and is not considered appropriate electronic business communication.

4. Bear in mind that some personal use of your organization's e-mail system may be warranted. American workers today put in more on-the-job hours than at any time in history. For employees who leave the house before dawn and don't return until well past dark, e-mail may be the most efficient and effective way to stay in touch with family members. For the sake of employee morale and retention, savvy employers generally are willing to accommodate their employees' need to check in electronically with children and spouses. Let your employees know where you stand on this issue, and how much personal use (if any) is acceptable.

5. Incorporate an overview of your organization's discrimination and sexual harassment policies within your e-mail policy. Because of the relaxed, informal nature of e-mail, some employees will put in writing comments they never would say aloud. Make sure employees understand that regardless of how it is transmitted, an inappropriate comment is an inappropriate comment. All it takes is one offensive message to land you on the wrong side of an expensive, protracted lawsuit.

6. Review your written e-policies with all employees. New hires and long-time employees, managers and supervisors, full-time professionals and part-time staff, telecommuters and temporary employees, independent contractors and freelancers—everyone should be informed of your e-mail, Internet, and software usage policies. Have all employees sign and date a copy of each policy to confirm they have read and understand each document.

7. Incorporate your written e-policies into your organization's employee handbook and new-hire orientation materials. Have the organization's human resources director review the e-policy with every new employee.

8. Address ownership issues and privacy expectations. Let employees know that the contents of the e-mail system belong to the organization, not the individual user. If management monitors and reads employee e-mail, say so. Make sure employees understand that their e-mail can, and will, be read at any time without notice to or permission of the employee. If there is any chance you may want to monitor employees' home computers, make that clear as well.

9. Support your e-mail and Internet policies with e-writing and cyberlanguage policies designed to reduce risks by controlling content.

10. Establish netiquette policies for e-mail senders and receivers, both managers and staff.

11. Implement a risk management policy that incorporates e-mail

retention and deletion policies, password policies, and monitoring/filtering policies.

12. Establish a computer security policy. Put into place procedures and tools designed to keep unscrupulous hackers and internal saboteurs out of your system.

13. Install software to monitor and filter e-mail and Internet use.

14. Purchase cyberinsurance policies to help mitigate electronic risks.

15. Develop an e-crisis communications policy for dealing with the media and public should an e-disaster occur.

DON'T

1. Rely solely on e-mail to communicate your e-policies. Require each employee to read, sign, and date a hard copy of each policy. Do use e-mail messages, along with the company's Intranet system, to remind employees of your policies and management's commitment to enforcing them.

2. Expect employees to train themselves. Educate employees about the whats, whys, and hows of your e-policies. Make employees aware of their e-risks, e-rights, e-responsibilities, and the repercussions they will face for violating e-mail, Internet, and software usage policies.

3. Create separate policies for management. Establish corporate e-mail, Internet, and software policies, and insist that officers, managers, supervisors, and staff adhere to them. A supervisor who turns a blind eye to an employee's online gambling addiction, a manager who winks at departmentwide software piracy, a board member who sends risqué jokes to senior executives—all put the organization at risk.

4. Forget your international associates. If you do business or operate facilities abroad, incorporate a discussion about effective international e-communication in your e-mail policy.

5. Assign one individual the responsibility of single-handedly enforcing your organization's e-policies. Make all managers and supervisors aware of the important role they play when it comes to
monitoring employee behavior. Assign specific monitoring and
enforcement roles to HR and information management professionals.

6. Allow employees to dismiss the organization's e-policies as
insignificant or unenforceable. Make sure employees understand
that their computer activity will be monitored. Stress the fact
that e-policy violators will face disciplinary action that may
include termination. Let employees know you mean business by
enforcing your e-policies consistently.

E-Policy Development and Implementation Checklist for Employers

I. E-Risk Assessment Checklist

1. An e-policy team of experienced professionals, committed to drafting and implementing your e-policies in a timely manner, has been formed.   ___**Yes**   ___**No**

2. A white knight has been assigned to oversee the e-policy team and communicate the project's importance to senior management and employees.   ___**Yes**   ___**No**

3. You have created tools to involve managers in the e-policy planning process, in order to garner their support for the policies and their commitment to policy implementation.   ____**Yes**   ___**No**

4. Employees have been surveyed to determine how they are using, misusing, and perhaps abusing your computer assets.   ____**Yes**   ___**No**

5. You have established a timeline for development and implementation of your organization's e-mail, Internet, and software usage policies.   ____**Yes**   ___**No**

II. Cyberlaw Checklist

1. You have consulted an employment law or cyberlaw expert to ensure your e-policies address the organization's e-risks and adhere to federal and state laws.   ____Yes ____No

2. Employees have been informed of their electronic rights via a written policy.   ____Yes ____No

3. You have notified employees of your e-mail and Internet monitoring policy.   ____Yes ____No

4. Employees have been educated about copyright infringement, and you have incorporated a copyright statement into your e-policy.   ____Yes ____No

5. You have addressed confidentiality issues with employees and incorporated a trade secret statement in your e-policy.   ____Yes ____No

III. E-Risk Management Checklist

1. You have conducted a top-to-bottom assessment of your organization's e-risks and your ability to manage risks with informed people and effective software.   ____Yes ____No

2. You have established a written policy governing e-mail deletion and retention.   ____Yes ____No

3. Employees have been educated about the dangers of e-mail, and have been instructed to empty their e-mailboxes.   ____Yes ____No

4. You have established internal procedures to keep employee passwords and workstation computers secure.   ____Yes ____No

5. Monitoring and filtering software has been installed to ensure the appropriate use of e-mail and the Internet.   ____Yes ____No

IV. E-Security Checklist

1. Firewalls have been installed correctly. ____Yes ____No

2. Encryption coding and virus detection software have been installed to keep human intruders and electronic bugs at bay. ____Yes ____No

3. You have hired computer security experts (an in-house team or third-party consultants) to identify and shore up e-security problems. ____Yes ____No

4. You have established a policy of conducting periodic computer security audits, and upgrading security policies, procedures, tools, and software as necessary. ____Yes ____No

5. You have educated employees about hackers—who they are, how they operate, why employees need to be on guard, etc. ____Yes ____No

V. Cyberinsurance Checklist

1. You have consulted with an insurance broker experienced with cyberrisks and e-insurance products. ____Yes ____No

2. You have established a comprehensive cyberinsurance program to help limit liabilities and control e-risks specific to your company. ____Yes ____No

3. You are committed to keeping your insurance broker informed about computer system enhancements and any changes in the type of e-commerce you engage in. ____Yes ____No

4. Your cyberinsurance broker keeps you informed about new e-insurance products. ____Yes ____No

VI. E-Mail Policy Checklist

1. You have advised employees that e-mail is not always the most effective or appropriate way to communicate. You have counseled employees to think about message, audience, and goal before deciding on e-mail, a phone call, or a face-to-face meeting. ____Yes ____No

2. In your e-mail policy, you have established clear guidelines for sending and receiving e-mail attachments. ____Yes ____No

3. You have established writing guidelines to control e-mail content and improve the overall effectiveness of employees' writing. ____Yes ____No

4. In an effort to limit waste of employee time and computer resources, you have set guidelines for message forwarding and listserv participation. ____Yes ____No

5. You have implemented a netiquette policy for employees and managers. ____Yes ____No

VII. Internet Policy Checklist

1. You have created a written policy that prohibits employees from using the organization's computer assets to visit inappropriate sites, or upload or download objectionable material from the Internet. ____Yes ____No

2. Your employees understand that the organization's computer resources are not to be wasted, but are to be used strictly for approved business purposes. ____Yes ____No

3. In an effort to keep Internet copy clean and clear, you have established cyberlanguage and content guidelines for the Net. ____Yes ____No

4. Rather than leave Internet policy
compliance to chance, you have installed
Internet monitoring and filtering software.   ____**Yes**   ____**No**

5. You reinforce your Internet policy with
ongoing employee education.   ____**Yes**   ____**No**

VIII. Software Policy Checklist

1. You have adopted a strict antipiracy stance
within your organization.   ____**Yes**   ____**No**

2. Employees have received comprehensive
software piracy training. They understand
softlifting is a serious crime that can cost
them their jobs and put the company
at risk.   ____**Yes**   ____**No**

3. You have explained software piracy risks
to managers and supervisors. Your management team is committed to enforcing
a strict antipiracy policy.   ____**Yes**   ____**No**

4. You have provided managers with the
tools they need to educate employees and
answer common questions about softlifting.   ____**Yes**   ____**No**

IX. E-Writing and E-Formatting Policy Checklist

1. To help control electronic content, you
have imposed an electronic writing policy.   ____**Yes**   ____**No**

2. Before drafting your e-writing policy, you
surveyed managers and employees to deter-
mine writing strengths and weaknesses.   ____**Yes**   ____**No**

3. Your e-writing policy focuses on the ABCs
of electronic business writing.   ____**Yes**   ____**No**

4. Cyberlanguage is addressed in your
e-writing policy.   ____**Yes**   ____**No**

5. To help speed the writing process, your
e-writing policy includes a grammar and
mechanics refresher. ____Yes ____No

6. You use your e-writing policy to teach
employees how to format e-mail for
maximum effectiveness. ____Yes ____No

7. You have retained a professional writing
coach to introduce employees to your new
e-writing policy, while providing a refresher
on business writing basics and effective
electronic writing. ____Yes ____No

8. You have provided employees with dictionaries and writing manuals. ____Yes ____No

X. Training Policy Checklist

1. Before communicating your new e-policies
to employees, you rallied managers as
e-policy advocates and enforcers. ____Yes ____No

2. You have developed manager training tools
that recap e-risks; summarize the employee
audit findings; review netiquette guidelines;
answer employees' most common questions;
and provide a breakdown, by violation, of
the disciplinary action employees will face if
they fail to comply with the organization's
e-policies. ____Yes ____No

3. Every employee has signed a copy of each
e-policy. A master set of e-mail, Internet,
and software policies is kept in the
company's employee handbook. ____Yes ____No

4. You have created continuing education
tools to reinforce training and ensure
e-policy compliance. ____Yes ____No

XI. E-Crisis Communications Policy Checklist

1. You have incorporated an e-crisis
   communications policy into your
   overall e-policy.   ____Yes   ____No

2. Professionals have been assigned to draft
   the e-crisis plan and establish a crisis
   response team to mitigate the damage
   should the worst happen.   ____Yes   ____No

3. Your spokesperson has undergone media
   skills training, if necessary.   ____Yes   ____No

4. You review your e-crisis policy and train
   your crisis team annually.   ____Yes   ____No

Sample E-Mail, Internet, and Computer Use Policies

SAMPLE 1: Use of E-Mail, Network, and Internet/Intranet

ABC CORP provides employees with an e-mail system, a network connection, and Internet and Intranet access. This policy governs all use of ABC CORP's network, Internet/Intranet access, and e-mail system, whether at the head office or remote offices, and whether for electronic mail, chat rooms, the Internet, newsgroups, electronic bulletin boards, or the ABC CORP Intranet.

The e-mail system, network, and Internet/Intranet access are for official business only. Employees are authorized to access the Internet for personal business only during nonworking time, and in strict compliance with the other terms of this policy.

All information created, sent, or received via the e-mail system, network, Internet, or the Intranet is the property of ABC CORP. Employees should not have any expectation of privacy regarding such information. This includes all e-mail messages and all electronic files. The company reserves the right to, at any time and without notice, access, read and review, monitor, and copy all messages and files on its computer system as it deems necessary. When it believes necessary, ABC CORP may disclose text or images to law enforcement or other third parties without the employee's consent.

Use extreme caution to ensure that the correct e-mail address is used for the intended recipient(s). Employees are expected to follow the rules of netiquette, as outlined in the company's e-writing guidelines, and to produce messages that are effective and professional.

Any message or file sent via e-mail must have the employee's name attached. Personal e-mail accounts (such as Hotmail) are not permitted unless expressly authorized in advance by ABC CORP's Systems Administrator at our headquarters. No employee may use a password unless it has been disclosed in writing to ABC CORP's Systems Administrator. Alternative Internet Service Provider connections to ABC CORP's internal network are not permitted unless expressly authorized and properly protected by a firewall or other appropriate security device(s).

Files that are downloaded from the Internet must be scanned with virus detection software before being viewed or opened. Also, employees are reminded that information obtained from the Internet is not always reliable and should be verified for accuracy before it is used.

Employees may not use ABC CORP's e-mail system, network, or Internet/Intranet access for any of the following:

1. Downloading of any software without the prior written approval of ABC CORP's Systems Administrator. (See ABC CORP's policy entitled "Acquisition, Use, and Copying of Software.")

2. Dissemination or printing of copyrighted materials, including articles and software, in violation of copyright laws.

3. Sending, receiving, printing, or otherwise disseminating proprietary data, trade secrets, or other confidential information of ABC CORP in violation of company policy or written agreements.

4. Operating a business, usurping business opportunities, or soliciting money for personal gain, or searching for jobs outside ABC CORP.

5. Offensive or harassing statements or language, including disparagement of others based on their race, color, religion, national origin, veteran status, ancestry, disability, age, sex, or sexual orientation.

6. Sending or soliciting sexually oriented messages or images.

7. Visiting sites featuring pornography, terrorism, espionage, theft, or drugs.

8. Gambling or engaging in any other activity in violation of local, state, or federal law.

9. Unethical activities or content, or activities or content that could damage ABC CORP's professional reputation.

Managers are responsible for ensuring that their employees follow this policy. Any employee who learns of a violation of this policy should notify ABC CORP's Systems Administrator or Human Resource Manager at our headquarters. Any employee who violates this policy or uses ABC CORP's e-mail system, network, Internet, or Intranet access for improper purposes shall be subject to discipline, up to and including discharge.

Employee Acknowledgment

If you have any additional questions about the above policies, address them to the Systems Administrator before signing the following agreement:

I have read ABC CORP's policy on the use of e-mail, network, and Internet/Intranet and agree to abide by it. I understand that violation of any of the above policies may result in discipline, up to and including my termination.

_____   _____   _____

User Name (Printed)   User Signature   Date

Source: © 2000, Donald C. Slowik, Attorney at Law with Lane, Alton & Horst. For informational purposes only. Individual policies should be developed with assistance from competent legal counsel.

SAMPLE 2: Computer Network and the Internet Acceptable Use Policy

The Company (the "Company") is pleased to make available to |certain associates access to interconnected computer systems within the Company (the "Network") and to the world-wide network that provides various means of accessing significant and varied materials and opportunities (commonly known as the "Internet"). (This Policy applies to associates if and when they are granted access. That access may be granted to the extent that the Company determines appropriate, based on the associate's duties or other factors.)

In order for the Company to be able to continue to make its Network and the Internet access available, all associates must take responsibility for appropriate and lawful use of this access. Associates must understand that one associate's misuse of the Network and the Internet access may jeopardize the ability of all associates to enjoy this access. While the Company's management and Network administrators will make reasonable efforts to administer use of the Network and Internet access, they must have associate cooperation in exercising and promoting responsible use of this access.

This document is the Computer Network and the Internet Acceptable Use Policy (the "Policy") of the Company and also relates to Internet and other access or service providers (collectively, the "Provider") as they provide resources necessary for the Company to provide the Network and Internet access. Upon accepting your account information, you are agreeing to follow this Policy, and you will then be given the opportunity to enjoy Network and Internet access in your office.

If you have any questions about the provisions of this Policy, you should contact the person who has been designated in your office as the one to whom you may direct your questions. If any user (that is, you or anyone whom you allow to use your account—which itself is a violation) using your account violates this Policy, your access will be denied or withdrawn and you may be subject to additional disciplinary action.

1. Personal Responsibility

By accepting your account password and other information from the Company and accessing the Network or the Internet, you are agreeing not only to follow the rules in this Policy, but also you are agreeing to report any misuse of access to the Network or the Internet to the person designated by the Company for this reporting. Misuse means any violations of this Policy, or any other use that, while not included in this Policy, has the effect of harming another or another's property.

2. Term of the Permitted Use

After you have been granted access and as long as you follow this Policy, you will have Network and Internet access during the term of your employment with the Company. (Please be aware that the Company may suspend access at any time for technical, policy, or other reasons.)

3. Purpose and Use

The Company is providing you access to its Network and the Internet *only* for Company business purposes. If you have any doubt about whether a contemplated activity is appropriate for Company business purposes, you may consult with the person designated by the Company to help you decide if a use is appropriate.

4. Netiquette and Prohibited Activity

All users must abide by rules of network etiquette, which include being polite and using the Network and the Internet in a safe and legal manner. The Company or authorized Company officials will make a good faith judgment as to which materials, files, information, software, communications, and other content and activity are permitted and prohibited based on the following guidelines and under the particular circumstances. Among uses that are considered unacceptable and constitute a violation of this Policy are the following:

(a) Using, transmitting, receiving, or seeking inappropriate, offensive, swearing, vulgar, profane, suggestive, obscene, abusive, harassing, belligerent, threatening, defamatory (harming another's reputation by lies), or misleading language or materials.

(b) Revealing personal information such as your or another's home address, telephone number, or social security number.

(c) Making ethnic, sexual preference, or gender-related slurs or jokes.

(d) Uses or activities that violate the law or the Associate Handbook or encourage others to violate the law or the Associate Handbook. This includes, for example:

(i) Offering for sale or use any substance the possession or use of which is prohibited by Company policy or the Associate Handbook.

(ii) Without proper authorization, accessing, transmitting, receiving, or seeking confidential information about clients or associates.

(iii) Conducting unauthorized business.

(iv) Viewing, transmitting, downloading, or seeking obscene or pornographic materials or materials that violate or encourage others to violate the law.

(v) Intruding, or trying to intrude, into the folders, files, work, networks, or computers of others, or intercepting communications intended for others.

(vi) Downloading or transmitting confidential information or trade secrets.

(e) Uses that cause harm to others or damage to their property. This includes, for example:

(i) Downloading or transmitting copyrighted materials without permission from the owner of the copyright in those materials. Even if materials on the Network or the Internet are not marked with the copyright symbol, ©, you should assume that they are protected under copyright laws unless there is explicit permission on the materials to use them.

(ii) Using another's password or some other user identifier that misleads message recipients into believing that some-one other than you is communicating or otherwise using the other's access to the Network or the Internet.

(iii) Uploading a virus or other harmful component or cor-rupted data, or vandalizing any part of the Network.

(iv) Using any software on the Network other than that licensed or approved by the Company.

(f) Uses that jeopardize the security of access and of the Net-work or other networks on the Internet. For example, don't disclose or share your password with others, and don't imper-sonate another.

(g) Accessing or attempting to access controversial or offensive materials.

You are advised that access to the Network and the Internet may include the potential for access to materials inappropriate for use for Company business purposes, including materials that may be illegal, defamatory, inaccurate, or offensive. Cer-tain of these areas on the Internet may contain warnings as to their content, and users are advised to heed these warnings. Not all sites that may contain inappropriate material, however, will include warnings. You must take responsibility for your use of the Network and the Internet and stay away from these sites. If you find that other users are visiting offensive or harm-ful sites, you should report that use to the person designated by the Company.

(h) Commercial uses. For example, don't sell or buy anything over the Internet, don't solicit or advertise the sale of any goods or services (whether to one recipient or many, such as "junk e-mail"), and don't give others private information about yourself or others, including credit card numbers and social security numbers.

(i) Uses that waste limited resources. For example, don't waste toner or paper in printers, and don't send chain letters, even for noncommercial or apparently "harmless" purposes, as these, like e-mail with large graphic attachments and "junk e-mail," use up limited Network capacity resources. Only copy others on an e-mail who should be "in the loop" on that e-mail. Be careful with distribution lists, determining first whether it is appropriate for everyone on that list to receive the e-mail. Do not send "all hands" e-mails without first obtaining permission.

(j) Suggesting to other associates that they view, download, or seek materials, files, information, software, or other content that may be offensive, defamatory, misleading, infringing, or illegal.

5. Confidential Information

You may have access to confidential information of the Company, its associates, and clients of the Company. E-mail makes it very easy to send and receive information and attachments. It is also easy to send confidential e-mail to more than those you intended. If you have a business need to communicate confidential information within the Company, with permission of management, you may do so by e-mail, but only sending the e-mail to those who have a need to know the information, and marking it "CONFIDENTIAL." Company management may from time to time issue guidelines to those whose responsibilities include the internal e-mail communication of confidential information. Again, when in doubt, do not send it by e-mail. Memoranda and reports on paper, telephone calls, and face-to-face meetings should be used in some contexts, such as with respect to personnel matters.

6. Use and Maintenance of Equipment and Facilities

The Company may occasionally issue rules for use and maintenance of computers and other equipment. These include the following: Do not keep any liquids or magnets on or near your computer, as these can cause serious damage. All original software assigned to you must be available in your office when your system needs to be serviced—it may need to be reinstalled. When you have a computer problem, record **all** the details about the problem on the appropriate form. Do not remove any computer from the building without written permission from Company management. Do not attempt to install software that is not licensed or authorized by the Company. Do not transport disks back and forth. (Viruses can easily be picked up onto your computer or the Network from the Internet or other computers.) Keep equipment plugged into a surge protector at all times. Report any damage to equipment to the appropriate authorities.

7. Privacy

Network and Internet access is provided as a tool for Company business. The Company reserves the right to monitor, inspect, copy, review, and store at any time and without prior notice any and all usage of the Network and the Internet access and any and all materials, files, information, software, communications, and other content transmitted, received, or stored in connection with this usage. All such information, content, and files shall be and remain the property of the Company, and you should not have any expectation of privacy regarding those materials. Network administrators may review files and intercept communications for any reason, including, but not limited to, for purposes of maintaining system integrity and ensuring that users are using the system consistently with this Policy.

8. Failure to Follow Policy

Your use of the Network and the Internet is a privilege, not a right. If you violate this Policy, at a minimum you will be subject to having your access to the Network and the Internet terminated, which the Company may refuse to reinstate for the remainder of your tenure in the Company. You breach this Policy not only by affirmatively violating the above provisions, but also by failing to report any violations of this Policy by other users which come to your attention. Further, you violate this Policy if you permit another to use your account or password to access the Network or the Internet, including but not limited to someone whose access has been denied or terminated. If the person you allow to use your account violates this Policy using your account, it is considered to be the same as you violating this Policy. Both of you are then subject to the consequences of that violation. The Company may take other disciplinary action under Company policy. A violation of this Policy may also be a violation of the law and subject the user to investigation and criminal or civil prosecution.

9. Warranties and Indemnification

The Company makes no warranties of any kind, either express or implied, in connection with its provision of access to or use of its Network or the Internet. It shall not be responsible for any claims, losses, damages, or costs (including attorneys' fees) of any kind suffered, directly or indirectly, by any user arising out of the user's use of, or inability to use, the Network or the Internet. By using the Network or the Internet, you are taking full responsibility for your use, and are agreeing to indemnify and hold harmless the Company, the Provider, and all of their directors, officers, members, managers, and employees from any and all loss, costs, claims, or damages (including reasonable attorneys' fees) resulting from access to and use of the Network or the Internet through your account, including but not limited to any fees or charges incurred through purchases of goods or services by the user. You agree to cooperate with the Company in the event of the Company's initiating an investigation of use or access to the Network or the Internet through your account, whether that use is on a Company computer or on another's outside the Network.

10. Updates

You may be asked from time to time to provide new or additional registration and account information, for example, to reflect developments in the law or technology. You must provide this information if you wish to continue to receive service. If after you have provided your account information, some or all of the information changes, you must notify the person designated by the Company to receive this information. This Policy may also be updated by the Company from time to time, for example, to reflect developments in the law or technology.

SAMPLE 3: Voice Mail and Computer Access Policy

ABC Company uses a voice mail system and supplies each employee with a voice mail box for business use. ABC Company may access all voice mail at any time for any reason without notice to individual users. No one should expect voice mail confidentiality or privacy vis-à-vis authorized Company personnel. The Network Administrator should be provided with access codes or passwords for use in such emergencies.

E-mail, the computer systems, and Internet also are to be used for Company business. E-mail is an efficient way to send urgent messages or those designed to reach multiple people simultaneously. Use extreme caution to ensure that the correct e-mail address is used for the intended recipient(s).

ABC Company may access and monitor e-mail at any time for any reason without notice. You should not expect or treat e-mail as confidential or private. E-mail users must provide the Network Administrator with passwords. Except for authorized Company personnel, no one is permitted to access another person's e-mail without consent.

System users should exercise judgment and common sense when distributing messages. Client-related messages should be carefully guarded and protected, like any other written materials. You must also abide by copyright laws, ethics rules, and other applicable laws.

Sending harassing, abusive, intimidating, discriminatory, or other offensive e-mails is strictly prohibited (see the Company's policy against sexual and other unlawful harassment). The use of the system to solicit for any purpose without the consent of the Human

Resources Director is strictly prohibited. Violation of this policy will subject employees to discipline up to and including termination.

Source: © 2000, Carlile Patchen & Murphy, LLP. Prepared by Attorney Marie-Joëlle C. Khouzam. For informational purposes only. No reliance should be placed on this without the advice of counsel.

SAMPLE 4: Policy Regarding Use of Voice Mail, E-Mail, and Other Company Equipment

The Company's voice mail, computer, and electronic mail systems are designed to assist us in better serving customers, enhancing internal communications, and reducing unnecessary paperwork. These guidelines should govern your use of company equipment, with special attention to e-mail:

1. Privacy is not assured in e-mail or voice mail messages, whether a password is used or not. The Systems Administrator must have access to passwords at all times, to ensure necessary access to the system. Misuse of passwords or the unauthorized use of another employee's password will result in disciplinary action, up to and including termination. The Company may access all employees' messages at any time.

2. Confidential information never should be sent over the Internet without the knowledge that it can be intercepted. This includes the transmission of documents containing customer financial information or Social Security numbers. Use extreme caution to ensure that the correct e-mail address is used for the intended recipient(s).

3. E-mail messages are like paper documents: Ask yourself whether you would want anyone else knowing about the content, or whether a conversation would be more appropriate.

4. E-mail usage must conform with the Company's policies against harassment and discrimination. Messages containing defamatory, obscene, offensive, or harassing information, or messages that disclose personal information without authorization, are prohibited. If you receive such unsolicited messages, you are to delete them

promptly and not forward them. Chain-type messages and executable graphics files also should be deleted and not forwarded—they cause overload on our system. Anyone engaging in the transmission of inappropriate e-mails, as determined by the Company, will be subject to discipline, up to and including termination. For further information regarding the Company's policy against sexual and other unlawful harassment, refer to your employee manual.

5. When using e-mail, you should use "e-mail etiquette." For example, avoid the use of all capital letters, as this is considered to be shouting at someone electronically.

6. If you create private mail groups, it is your responsibility to review them periodically so they remain current. The Company's Systems Administrator will have responsibility for generating and maintaining public mail distribution lists.

7. You should be mindful of Company policies regarding e-mail retention periods. It is your responsibility to archive any messages that you do not wish to be automatically deleted.

8. E-mail and Internet access should not be overused or misused. Misuse of electronic access (i.e., work time spent online, copying or downloading copyrighted materials, visiting inappropriate sites) will result in discipline.

Thank you for your cooperation in properly using the Company's resources. Questions regarding this policy and/or e-mail usage should be directed to the Human Resources Director or Systems Administrator.

Source: © 2000, Carlile Patchen & Murphy, LLP. Prepared by Attorney Marie-Joëlle C. Khouzam. For informational purposes only. No reliance should be placed on this without the advice of counsel.

Sample 5: Computer Use Policy

This memorandum sets forth (the company's) policy with regard to access to and disclosure of electronic data created or stored by the company employees using the company's computer system.

Electronic data as used here, <u>includes electronic mail messages</u> sent or received by company employees with the use of the company's electronic mail system. *Electronic data* also refers to <u>any document or file</u> created using application software or a text-editing program. *Computer system* refers to all company-owned portable, laptop, notebook, palmtop, stand-alone, and networked computers.

The company intends to honor these policies but must reserve the right to change them at any time with such prior notice, if any, as may be reasonable under the circumstances.

1. Regulated Uses of the Computer System

The company reserves the right to access and disclose all electronic files on the computer system, for any purpose.

Incidental and occasional personal use of computers is permitted within the company, with permission of the office manager. Electronic files created for personal use will be treated no differently from other electronic data.

2. Use by Third Parties

Only company employees may use the company's electronic mail system.

3. No Intrusive Review of Data Permitted

It is a violation of company policy for any employee, including system administrators and supervisors, to use the electronic mail and computer systems for purposes of satisfying idle curiosity about the affairs of others, with no substantial business purpose for obtaining access to the files or communications of others.

Such intrusive behavior will be considered grounds for discipline and/or termination of employment.

4. Monitoring for Policy Compliance

Management may conduct random audits of data files and electronic mail communications to determine whether there have been any breaches of security or violations of company policy on the part of employees.

5. Grounds for Targeted Access

The company reserves the right to access and disclose the contents of employee electronic files, including electronic mail communications, but will do so only when it has a legitimate business need to do so.

6. Use of Information Gained by Targeted Access

The contents of data files, including electronic mail communications, properly obtained for legitimate business purposes, may be disclosed within the company without the permission of the employee.

Any internal disclosure without the employee's consent shall be limited to those employees who have some reasonable need for access to the information.

7. Disclosure to Third Parties

The company may disclose the contents of electronic data files for any business purpose.

The company will attempt to refrain from disclosure of particular messages, based on objections on the grounds that publication of the message will create personal embarrassment for the employee who created/sent the file, unless such disclosure is required to serve an important business purpose or satisfy a legal obligation.

Sample E-Risk Management Policy

A. Background

The purpose of this guideline is to establish appropriate parameters for the management of the vast amounts of electronic data regularly produced and backed up by COMPANY employees, and to alert all employees to the risks associated with the retention of electronic data not constituting the official position of the company. Further, the guideline addresses the responsibilities of COMPANY systems administrators and end users in implementing these recommendations.

B. Management of Corporate (Official) Records

Official records reflect the final, official recorded position of an organization related to the specific content of the record. Official records reflect the intent of the organization. From a court perspective, organizations will likely attempt to introduce records as "business records" under the "Rules of Evidence." Official records must therefore be subject to rigorous procedures for creation and destruction under a records management or records retention program.[1]

It is the policy of COMPANY to establish a Corporate Records Management Program throughout the company to comply with all legal requirements, government regulations, and the business and operational needs of the company. The Corporate Records

Management Program shall provide a method of identifying, maintaining, protecting, retaining, and disposing of company records.

The COMPANY Disaster Recovery Planning Unit–Corporate Records Administrator prepares, publishes, and maintains a "Corporate Records Management Manual" containing the program requirements and procedures. Each Division Manager is responsible for ensuring compliance within their respective division for all procedures and requirements of the Corporate Records Program as established. Division Managers should familiarize themselves with the Records Retention Schedules to identify Corporate (Official) Records affecting their respective divisions.

C. Identifying Unofficial Electronic Records

Unofficial records include drafts, work-in-progress items, copies of records, electronic records used to create official signed documents, unsigned letters, and other material that is either in a preliminary state of development or has not yet been authorized or approved by an appropriate person. These unofficial electronic records do not yet reflect the official position of the organization or remain subject to change before completion.

Unofficial electronic records are created in a variety of formats, including, but not limited to:

1. Word processing documents and text (ASCI) files;

2. Electronic mail messages and groupware objects and items, e.g., attachments, calendars, schedules, task lists, distribution lists, etc. E-mail/groupware storage mechanisms, such as bulletin boards, "folders" and "outboxes," and Lotus Notes databases;

3. Spreadsheet files;

4. Database records (stand alone and distributed, i.e., client-server);

5. Image files and microfiche/film, not constituting corporate (official) records;

6. Other data types including video, sound, etc.;

7. Data backed up from the server or local PC/workstation, including back-up logs;

8. Data salvageable (recoverable even after deletion) either on the server or PC desktop;

9. Network system, security system, and audit trail logs;

10. User IDs and passwords; and

11. Voice mail messages (At this time, COMPANY voice mail is not backed up, although "read" and not deleted voice mail is discoverable. Recovery of voice mail items may be required via Telecommunications.)

The electronic data formats noted above can be stored in a variety of locations, including the network, local PC hard drives, floppy disks, CD-ROM or optical disks, magnetic tapes [including digital audio tapes (DAT)], or even mainframe disk packs. Data derived from phone systems, fax machines, and Personal Digital Assistants (PDAs) also are included.

D. Need for Management of Unofficial Electronic Records

Even though unofficial electronic records need not be subject to the same rigorous procedures as official corporate records, a general records retention guideline specifies its management. Such a guideline is important to COMPANY to better manage and control the growing amount of inactive and obsolete data. Considerable computer and staff resources are required to store and back up this data. In addition, it is far more time consuming and costly to produce final work products (i.e., official records), when electronic data is unorganized.

Also, computerized files are increasingly a prime target for subpoenas (from both government and private litigants), discovery requests or demands, search warrants, and electronic surveillance. With changing discovery rules, rapid accumulation of electronic data, the growing and uncontrolled use of electronic mail, and the increased use of backup and archive systems, the problem will intensify in the coming years.

Further, recent federal rulings, *Federal Rules of Civil Procedure 26(a) and 16(b)*, which took effect December 1, 1993, have profound implications for litigants (i.e., COMPANY) who use computers. The new rules require parties to a lawsuit to disclose, before discovery begins, the categories and locations of data compilations that may be relevant to the specific matters raised in the complaint. For example, when corporate counsel or business staff at COMPANY receive a subpoena for document requests, corporate counsel is required by law to furnish <u>all</u> data relevant to the request, including electronic data that is backed up, salvageable, and retained by both legal and related business areas. Electronic records, particularly word processing documents and electronic mail messages, often contain early drafts and "off-the-cuff" remarks that can be misleading if taken out of context in litigation.

Complying with discovery requests can prove burdensome and costly, both in computer and staff time, where electronic data is not organized in a useful way, or not easily accessible. Further, the typical end user is unaware that the "delete key" does not in fact <u>delete</u> that data for all purposes; believing the data in question to be gone, the end user will not know to consult the systems administrator, and material subject to discovery may be inadvertently withheld.

E. Records Retention Guideline for Unofficial Electronic Records

Thus, it is inadvisable for a number of reasons to retain and track every electronic data item. Instead, the electronic data should be evaluated to determine how long it should be retained, how it can be organized and how it can be most efficiently retrieved. The following guidelines are recommended for managing electronic data and minimizing litigation risk. COMPANY systems administrators are responsible for:

1. **Understanding this policy and distributing it to their staff and end users** whom they support. In particular, managers

must be sure that all end-users are familiar with backup procedures in the area, and understand that use of the "delete" instruction does not always mean a purge of the data. All questions regarding compliance should be directed to COMPANY counsel (Law Area).

2. Identifying all **electronic media sources**, such as magnetic disks, tape, diskettes, optical disks, or other storage media. All media where corporate data is stored, whether on diskettes or mainframe disk packs, at work or at home, is discoverable and must be produced upon request.

3. Identifying how the **unofficial electronic records** are structured and organized. For example, what is the directory (local or networked) structure for all users when producing word processing documents? What file servers do these documents reside on? Are users also using diskettes to store their material? Where are electronic mail items stored? Where can electronic mail items be saved or archived by the user?

4. Identifying all tape or optical **backup resources** where the unofficial electronic records may reside. As noted in the example above, where are all word processing documents or electronic mail messages backed up? Are there multiple backup copies, i.e., local backup tapes of standalone PCs/workstations, on-site, off-site, and a disaster recovery hot site? What is the backup schedule? Are there full or incremental backups, and when? Are backup media destroyed after six months, one year? In addition, some programs, such as WordPerfect, can create a "timed backup" of a document for recovery in the event of PC or network failure. Knowledge of such application features and knowing where the "files" are created and maintained is required.

5. Reviewing **salvageable electronic data.** In traditional PC-based architectures, when an electronic file is erased it usually only deletes the reference to its location on the disk. The computer then treats the space taken up by the old file as available and may write over it. Until the information has been overwrit-

ten, however, it can be retrieved using special programs. Awareness of the various Windows and DOS-based restoration facilities used in the systems support area is required, along with how the Novell NetWare–based "salvage" feature is deployed.

6. Producing **each** unofficial record as identified above in a format as might be requested by COMPANY counsel in connection with a subpoena, including:

   a. Classifying and indexing electronic information;

   b. Printing electronic data; and

   c. Copying electronic data on appropriate storage media, e.g., magnetic diskettes, optical CDs, etc.

7. Providing PC and network access to government and law enforcement officials, i.e., Federal Marshals, FBI, SEC, etc., as might be requested and supervised by COMPANY counsel.

All COMPANY systems administrators <u>must</u>:

1. **Review and document the records retention program for their respective information systems at least once a year** to ensure timely compliance with these requirements.

2. In consultation with their end-users, carefully examine their data backup systems/schemes and weigh the burden, in time and money, of having to reproduce electronic data against the risks associated with unmanaged backup. In any event, **data backups for unofficial electronic records should never exceed one year. Data on backup media exceeding one year should be destroyed**.

3. Be ready and willing to discuss their information systems structures with their users and/or COMPANY counsel at any given time.

4. Be ready and willing to assist COMPANY's Auditing division with any requests to ensure compliance with this guideline.

All COMPANY employees <u>must</u> comply with the items below:

1. **Unofficial electronic records must be destroyed as soon as possible when superseded, when the information has been transcribed to another record, or when no longer useful. The unofficial record should not be retained longer than the official version.**

2. An electronic data review and cleanup should be performed periodically. It is best to perform such a **cleanup each year in the first quarter** to discard data records (i.e., e-mail and documents) that no longer serve any useful purpose.

F. Employee Action to Take When Subpoenaed

No employee shall provide corporate data to private litigants or others without the consent of COMPANY Law Area counsel. All requests for information from outside sources and all questions regarding this policy should be forwarded to COMPANY counsel. COMPANY counsel also is available to discuss litigation-sensitive issues.

If an employee receives a request to produce electronic records, the employee shall not attempt to destroy any electronic data he or she feels relates to the request. A corporation has a duty to identify and preserve electronic data to avoid charges of destruction of evidence.

As such, any electronic records that relate to a pending or threatened legal proceeding or investigation should be retained until COMPANY counsel advises that retention is no longer necessary, notwithstanding any guidelines above to the contrary.

COMPANY systems administrators should become familiar with this guideline. Any questions regarding this guideline should be directed to COMPANY counsel in the Law Area. Systems administrators may be called upon to support COMPANY counsel in future discovery requests.

Sample Software Usage Policies

SAMPLE 1: Corporate Policy Statement

Company/Agency Policy Regarding the Use of Personal Computer Software

(Company/Agency) licenses the use of copies of computer software from a variety of outside companies. (Company/Agency) does not own the copyright to this software or its related documentation and, except for a single copy for backup purposes or unless expressly authorized by the copyright owner(s), does not have the right to reproduce it for use on more than one computer.

With regard to software usage on local area networks, (Company/Agency) shall use the software only in accordance with the license agreement.

(Company/Agency) employees are not permitted to install their own copies of any software onto (Company/Agency) machines. (Company/Agency) employees are not permitted to copy software from (Company/Agency's) computers and install it on home or any other computers.

(Company/Agency) employees, learning of any misuse of software or related documentation within the company, shall notify the Manager of Computer Systems or other appropriate person. According to the U.S. and Canadian copyright law, unauthorized reproduction of software is a federal offense. Offenders can be subject to civil damages of as much as U.S. $100,000 per title copied, and criminal penalties, including fines (up to U.S. $250,000 per work copied, CN $1,000,000) and imprisonment (up to 5 years per title copied).

Any (Company/Agency) employee who knowingly makes, acquires, or uses unauthorized copies of computer software licensed to (Company/Agency) or who places or uses unauthorized software on (Company/Agency) premises or equipment shall be subject to immediate termination of employment.

(Company/Agency) does not condone and specifically forbids the unauthorized duplication of software.

I am fully aware of the software protection policies of (Company/Agent) and agree to uphold those policies.

Employee Signature and Date

Source: Software & Information Industry Association (SIIA), SPA Anti-Piracy Division.

SAMPLE 2: Employee Internet Usage Policy

As part of this organization's commitment to the utilization of new technologies, many/all of our employees have access to the Internet. In order to ensure compliance with the copyright law, and protect ourselves from being victimized by the threat of viruses or hacking into our server, the following is effective immediately:

1. It is (Organization's) policy to limit Internet access to official business. Employees are authorized to access the Internet for personal business after-hours, in strict compliance with the other terms of this policy. The introduction of viruses, or malicious tampering with any computer system, is expressly prohibited. Any such activity will immediately result in termination of employment.

2. Employees using (Organization's) accounts are acting as representatives of (Organization). As such, employees should act accordingly to avoid damaging the reputation of the organization.

3. Files that are downloaded from the Internet must be scanned

with virus detection software before installing or execution. All appropriate precautions should be taken to detect for a virus and, if necessary, to prevent its spread.

4. The truth or accuracy of information on the Internet and in e-mail should be considered suspect until confirmed by a separate (reliable) source.

5. Employees shall not place company material (copyrighted software, internal correspondence, etc.) on any publicly accessible Internet computer without proper permission.

6. Alternate Internet Service Provider connections to (Organization's) internal network are not permitted unless expressly authorized and properly protected by a firewall or other appropriate security device(s).

7. The Internet does not guarantee the privacy and confidentiality of information. Sensitive material transferred over the Internet may be at risk of detection by a third party. Employees must exercise caution and care when transferring such material in any form.

8. Unless otherwise noted, all software on the Internet should be considered copyrighted work. Therefore, employees are prohibited from downloading software and/or modifying any such files without permission from the copyright holder.

9. Any infringing activity by an employee may be the responsibility of the organization. Therefore, this organization may choose to hold the employee liable for the employee's actions.

10. This organization reserves the right to inspect an employee's computer system for violations of this policy.

I have read (organization's) anti-piracy statement and agree to abide by it as consideration for my continued employment by (organization). I understand that violation of any above policies may result in my termination.

_____   _____
(User Signature)   (Date)

Source: Software & Information Industry Association (SIIA), SPA Anti-Piracy Division.

SAMPLE 3: Guidelines for Organization Software Use

General Statement of Policy

It is the policy of (organization) to respect all computer software copyrights and to adhere to the terms of all software licenses to which (organization) is a party. (Organization) will take all steps necessary to prohibit users from duplicating any licensed software or related documentation for use either on (organization) premises or elsewhere unless (organization) is expressly authorized to do so by agreement with the licenser. Unauthorized duplication of software may subject user and/or (organization) to both civil and criminal penalties under the United States Copyright Act. (Organization) must not permit any employee to use software in any manner inconsistent with the applicable license agreement, including giving or receiving software or fonts from clients, contractors, customers and others.

User Education

(Organization) must provide and require a software education program for all its software users (to be crafted by the software manager). Upon completion of the education program, users are required to sign the (organization's) Employee Personal Computer Software Usage Guidelines. New users will be provided the same education program within ten (10) days of the commencement date of their employment.

Budgeting for Software

When acquiring computer hardware, software, and training, (organization) must budget accordingly to meet the cost at the time of acquisition. When purchasing software for existing computers, (organization) must charge the purchases to the department's budget for information technology or an appropriate budget set aside for tracking software purchases.

Acquisition of Software

All software acquired by (organization) must be purchased through the (MIS, purchasing, or other appropriate designated) department. Software may not be purchased through user corporate credit cards, petty cash, travel, or entertainment budgets. Software acquisition channels are restricted to ensure that (organization) has a complete record of all software that has been purchased for (organization) computers and can register, support, and upgrade such software accordingly. This includes software that may be downloaded and/or purchased from the Internet.

Registration of Software

When (organization) receives the software, the designated department (MIS, purchasing, etc.) must receive the software first to complete registration and inventory requirements before installation. In the event the software is shrink-wrapped, the designated department is responsible for completing the registration card and returning it to the software publisher. Software must be registered in the name of (organization) and the department in which it will be used. Due to personnel turnover, software never will be registered in the name of the individual user. The designated department maintains a register of all (organization's) software and will keep a library of software licenses. The register must contain:

(a) the title and publisher of the software;

(b) the date and source of software acquisition;

(c) the location of each installation as well as the serial number of the hardware on which each copy of the software is installed;

(d) the existence and location of backup copies; and

(e) the software product's serial number.

Installation of Software

After the registration requirements above have been met, the software will be installed by the software manager. Once installed, the original media will be kept in a safe storage area maintained by the designated department. User manuals, if provided, will reside either with the user or the software manager.

Home Computers

(Organization's) computers are organization-owned assets and must be kept both software legal and virus free. Only software purchased through the procedures outlined above may be used on (organization's) machines. Users are not permitted to bring software from home and load it onto (organization's) computers. Generally, organization-owned software cannot be taken home and loaded on a user's home computer if it also resides on (organization's) computer. If a user is to use software at home, (organization) will purchase a separate software package and record it as an organization-owned asset in the software register. However, some software companies provide in their license agreements that home use is permitted under certain circumstances. If a user needs to use software at home, he/she should consult with the software manager or designated department to determine if appropriate licenses permit home use.

Shareware

Shareware software is copyrighted software that is distributed via the Internet. It is the policy of (organization) to pay shareware authors the fee that they specify for use of their product. Under this policy, acquisition and registration of shareware products will be handled the same as commercial software products.

Quarterly Audits

The software manager or designated department will conduct a quarterly audit of all (organization's) PCs and servers, including portables, to ensure that (organization) is in compliance with all software licenses. Surprise audits may be conducted as well. Audits will be conducted using an auditing software product. Also, during the quarterly audit, (organization) will search for computer viruses and eliminate any that are found. The full cooperation of all users is required during audits.

Penalties and Reprimands

According to the U.S. Copyright Act, illegal reproduction of software is subject to civil damages of as much as U.S. $100,000 per title infringed, and criminal penalties, including fines of as much as U.S. $250,000 per title infringed, and imprisonment of up to five years. An (organization) user who makes, acquires, or uses unauthorized copies of software will be disciplined as appropriate under the circumstances. Such discipline may include termination of employment. (Organization) does not condone the illegal duplication of software and will not tolerate it.

I have read (organization's) antipiracy statement and agree to bind the (organization) accordingly. I understand that violation of any above policies may result in both civil liability and criminal penalties for the (organization) and/or its employees.

Signature

Title

Date

Source: Software & Information Industry Association (SIIA), SPA Anti-Piracy Division.

SAMPLE 4: Guidelines for Employee Software Use

Software will be used only in accordance with its license agreement. Unless otherwise provided in the license, any duplication of copyrighted software, except for backup and archival purposes by the software manager or designated department, is a violation of copyright law. In addition to violating copyright law, unauthorized duplication of software is contrary to (organization's) standards of conduct. The following points are to be followed to comply with software license agreements:

1. All users must use all software in accordance with license agreements and the (organization's) software policy. All users acknowledge that they do not own this software or its related documentation, and, that unless expressly authorized by the software publisher, may not make additional copies except for archival purposes.

2. (Organization) will not tolerate the use of any unauthorized copies of software or fonts in our organization. Any person illegally reproducing software can be subject to civil and criminal penalties including fines and imprisonment. Users must not condone illegal copying of software under any circumstances. Anyone who makes, uses, or otherwise acquires unauthorized software will be appropriately disciplined.

3. No user will give software or fonts to any outsiders, including clients, customers, and others. Under no circumstances will (organization) use software that has been brought in from any unauthorized location under (organization's) policy, including, but not limited to, the Internet, home, friends, and colleagues.

4. Any user who determines that there may be a misuse of software within the organization will notify the Certified Software Manager, department manager, or legal counsel.

5. All software used by (organization) on (organization)-owned computers will be purchased through appropriate procedures.

I have read (organization's) software code of ethics. I am fully aware of our software compliance policies and agree to abide by them. I understand that violation of any above policies may result in my termination.

_____

Employee Signature

_____

Date

Source: Software & Information Industry Association (SIIA), SPA Anti-Piracy Division.

SAMPLE 5: Guidelines for Employees' Home Software Use

Consistent with paragraph seven (7) of (Organization's) Software Use Guidelines, employee use of (organization's) software at home is strictly prohibited unless express permission is received from (organization's) software manager or designated department. If the software manager or designated department determines home use is permissible under the relevant software license agreement, then in exchange for the privilege of home use, I expressly agree to the following terms and conditions of home software use:

1. To install only the permissible number of copies of (organization's) software into my home computer as determined by (organization's) software manager or designated department under the relevant software license agreement.

2. To use the (organization's) software consistently with the software's license agreement and (organization's) software policy, including, but not limited to, restricting the software's use to (organization's) business only.

3. To subject my home computer with (organization's) software for periodic software audits to ensure the (organization's) software compliance, consistent with paragraph nine (9) of (Organization's) Software Use Guidelines. (See Sample 3.)

4. To remove the (organization's) software from my computer and return materials I may have relating to (organization's) software back to (organization) should I cease to work for (organization). I understand that continued use of the software may subject me to potential civil liability.

I have read (organization's) Software Use Guidelines and the preceding terms applying to home use of (organization's) software. I am fully aware of the software compliance policies and agree to abide by them. I understand that violation of any of the (organization's) software use policies, including, but not limited to, the terms above, may result in my termination.

_____

Employee Signature

_____

Date

Source: Software & Information Industry Association (SIIA), SPA Anti-Piracy Division.

SAMPLE 6: Acquisition, Use, and Copying of Software

ABC CORP will acquire software only by purchasing it from authorized software distributors in accordance with the procedures set forth below. Further, it is ABC CORP's policy to respect all computer software copyrights and to adhere strictly to the terms of all software licenses to which it is a party.

Acquisition and Use of Software

Software acquisition channels are restricted to ensure that ABC CORP's Systems Administrator has a complete record of all software that has been purchased for ABC CORP computers and can register, support, and upgrade such software accordingly.

All software acquired by any ABC CORP office must be purchased through the Systems Administrator. Submit a Purchase Order to the Systems Administrator, and he/she will arrange for approval of the Purchase Order, payment, and delivery of the software.

1. No software may be purchased by using corporate credit cards, petty cash, travel, or entertainment budgets, etc.

2. No software may be acquired or used for "alpha" testing, demonstration, or other trial purposes, without the advance written approval of the Systems Administrator.

3. No shareware or other "Public Domain" software may be acquired or used without the advance written approval of the Systems Administrator. Shareware software is copyrighted software that is distributed freely through bulletin boards and online services. It is the policy of ABC CORP to pay shareware authors the fee they specify for use of their products. Registration of shareware products will be handled the same way as commercial software products.

4. No software or program coding is to be downloaded from an external source, without the advance written approval of the Systems Administrator.

5. No employee-owned software may be installed on ABC CORP equipment without the advance written approval of the Systems Administrator.

6. No ABC CORP software may be given to any non-ABC CORP users, including clients, contractors, customers, and others.

7. No ABC CORP software may used in violation of the software's license agreement. This includes use of the software on local area networks and on multiple machines.

All software purchased for ABC CORP or its branch offices will be shipped directly to the Systems Administrator at our headquarters office, who will complete registration and inventory requirements. Software will be registered only in the name of ABC CORP and the job title or department in which it will be used. The Systems Administrator will maintain a register of all ABC CORP software and will keep a library of software licenses. The register must contain: (a) the title and publisher of the software; (b) the date and source of software acquisition; (c) the location of each installation as well as the identification number of the hardware on which each copy of the software is installed; (d) the name of the authorized user; (e) the existence and location of any backup copies; (f) the software product's serial number. Due to personnel turnover, software never will be registered in the name of the individual user.

When software has been purchased for the headquarters office of ABC CORP, the Systems Administrator will install the software and keep the original software (and any authorized backup copies) in a secured and locked area.

When software has been purchased for other offices of ABC CORP, the Systems Administrator will make and keep any authorized backup copies, and then will send the original software and instructions to the particular ABC CORP office for installation. After installation, the office must keep the original software in a secured and locked area as instructed by the Systems Administrator. No other installation or copying of the software may occur without the advance written approval of the Systems Administrator or, in the event of an emergency, his or her supervisor.

Use on Home Computers

Generally, ABC CORP–owned software cannot be taken home and loaded on an employee's home computer if it also resides on an ABC CORP computer. If an employee is required to use software at home, ABC CORP will purchase a separate package and record it as an organization-owned asset in the software register. However, some software companies provide in their license agreements that home use is permitted under certain circumstances. If an employee is required to use software at home, he or she must first consult with the Systems Administrator to determine if appropriate licenses allow for home use.

Copying or Alteration of Software

The copying of software by anyone other than the Systems Administrator is strictly prohibited. The Systems Administrator will create and keep any backup copies of software allowed by law.

No ABC CORP employee may alter any licensed software or related documentation, for use either on company premises or elsewhere, unless ABC CORP is expressly authorized to do so by agreement with the licenser.

Unauthorized duplication or alteration of software will subject individual users to disciplinary action, up to and including discharge, and may result in civil or criminal penalties under the U.S. Copyright Act.

Employee's Duty to Report Violations

ABC CORP employees learning of any acquisition, use, or copying of software in violation of this policy shall notify their department manager or the Systems Administrator immediately.

Audits and Enforcement

Department managers and team leaders will be responsible for enforcing this policy in their organizations. The Systems Administrator will have sole responsibility for the interpretation of this policy. The Systems Administrator will be responsible for providing guidance to the requirements of this policy and for conducting periodic audits to ensure compliance with this policy.

The Systems Administrator will conduct at least annual audits of ABC CORP's computing equipment, including portable computers, to ensure compliance with all software licenses. Surprise audits may be conducted as well. Audits may be conducted using an auditing software product. Also, during the audits, the Systems Administrator may search for computer viruses and eliminate any that are found. The full cooperation of all users is required during audits.

Employee Acknowledgment

If you have any additional questions about the above policies, address them to the Systems Administrator before signing the following agreement.

I have read ABC CORP's policy on the acquisition, use, and copying of software, and agree to abide by it. I understand that violation of any of the above policies may result in discipline, up to and including my termination.

_____

User Name (Printed)

_____

User Signature

_____

Date

Source: © 2000, Donald C. Slowik, Attorney at Law with Lane, Alton & Horst. For informational purposes only. Individual policies should be developed with assistance from competent legal counsel.

Glossary of Computer and Electronic Writing Terms

Acronym[1] A word formed from the first letters of a phrase's words. Example: "LOL" for "laughing out loud."

Active File An electronic data file that has not been deleted or otherwise destroyed and/or damaged. An active file is readily visible to the operating system and/or the software with which it was created.

Active Verb A verb that expresses an action. Examples: *Write*, *train*, and *enforce*.

Active Voice The most powerful way to write. In the active voice, the subject (the actor) of the verb (the action) is also the subject of the sentence. Example: *The manager* (the actor) *monitors* (the action) *employee e-mail on an as-needed basis.*

Address The destination of an e-mail message.

Address Book An electronic collection of e-mail addresses.

Antecedent Noun The noun for which a pronoun is substituted. Example: *The marketing director* (antecedent noun) *was shocked when the confidential e-mail message he* (pronoun) *sent his wife appeared on his colleagues' computer screens.*

Archiving   Storing old e-mail messages that warrant neither attention nor deletion.

Article   The words *a, an, the.*

Attachment   A computer file sent with an e-mail message. The file can be a word processing document, spreadsheet, database, or graphic element.

Back up   Saving data to an external source such as a diskette or tape.

Bcc   Blind carbon copy.

Cc   Carbon copy.

Cliché   An overused word or phrase that has become part of everyday language and adds fat to business writing.

Compression   A file management technique that shrinks data for easy transportation and storage.

Contraction   A word formed by combining two words and replacing one or more letters with an apostrophe. Example: *It's* for *it is.*

Coordinating Conjunction   A part of speech (*and, or, nor, for, but, so, yet*) that connects words and groups of words of the same rank: nouns with nouns, verbs with verbs, independent clauses with independent clauses, etc.

Copyright   The exclusive right granted to authors under the U.S. Copyright Act to copy, adapt, distribute, rent, publicly perform, and publicly display their works of authorship, such as literary works, databases, musical works, sound recordings, photographs and other still images, and motion pictures and other audiovisual works.[2]

Counterfeiting (software)   Making, distributing, and/or selling software that is faked to look like the real thing.[3]

CPU   Abbreviation for "central processing unit," the brains of the computer.

Cracker   A malicious intruder who breaks into computers and systems to cause damage, typically motivated by power, greed, or revenge.

Crackz   Material or software designed to circumvent copyright protections to facilitate illegal software use.[4]

Cybercrisis   A high-profile electronic disaster that focuses the attention of the media and other important audiences on an organization.

Cyberextortionists   Hackers who threaten harm to computer systems and confidential information unless ransoms are paid.

Cyberfraud   An illegal computer scam or con game.

Cybergrammar   The correct use of mechanics (grammar, punctuation, and spelling) in electronic documents.

Cyberinsurance   Insurance products that are designed to reduce electronic risks in the workplace.

Cyberlanguage   The language employees use to communicate electronically. Within the confines of the organization's e-writing policy, the employer should establish cyberlanguage guidelines. Cyberlanguage should be businesslike and professional.

Cyberlaw   The practice of law concentrating on issues related to e-commerce and e-communication, including e-mail, Internet, and software policies.

Cyberslackers   Employees who log onto the Net and thereby slack off work during business hours.

Cyberspace   The electronic environment in which people communicate via computers.

Cyberthieves   Also known as hackers or crackers. Those who break into computer systems to steal funds or information.

Deleted File   An electronic data file that has been deleted or removed from the electronic media on which it resided.

Denial of Service   A malicious hacker attack. The deliberate attempt to shut down a network operation by overloading it.

Disk/Floppy Disk   A plastic or metallic object used to store computer data.

Dumpster Diving   Sorting through trash containers for information to ʌacilitate hacking or social engineering. It is popular with hackers.

Electronic Correspondence   E-mail messages and attachments.

Electronic Jargon   Acronyms, abbreviations, and slang used and understood by a limited number of e-mail users.

Electronic Shorthand   A means for e-mail writers to express emotion. It is not understood by all e-mail users. Example: <g> for "grin."

E-mail   An electronic message transmitted between computers.

Emoticons   Electronic symbols of emotion. Also called "smileys," emoticons are graphic renderings that are intended to substitute for body language and facial expressions. Tilt your head to the left to see a smile :) or a wink ;).

Encryption   The process of scrambling an e-mail message to ensure privacy. Once received, the message must be decoded by the recipient.

Executive Summary   Short section of copy preceding a lengthy or technical document. It highlights key points in conversational language.

E-zine   Original content that is published on a Web site. An electronic magazine.

Filing   The organization of active e-mail messages and/or files.

File Server   A computer workstation that serves stored data and files or processing power to other machines, or clients, on a network.[5]

Filter   An e-mail program feature that allows the user to sort incoming messages.

Firewall   The wall of software that keeps unauthorized users or intruders outside a network. A firewall may also keep company users from browsing the Web.

Five Ws   Who, what, when, where, and why; five questions to answer before starting to write.

Flame   An angry or insulting e-mail message.

Folder   Related computer messages and/or documents that are stored together.

Forward   Retransmitting one e-mail message to a second reader.

Freeware   Software, covered by copyright, for which copies can be made for archival and distribution purposes, but distribution cannot be for profit. Modifications to the software are allowed and encouraged. Decompiling, or reverse engineering, of the program code is allowed. Development of new works, or derivative works built on the package, is allowed as long as the derivative works are designated as freeware. In other words, you cannot take freeware, modify or extend it, then sell it as commercial or shareware software.[6]

Gender   The grammatical categories of masculine, feminine, or neuter.

Gender-Neutral Language   Words that indicate no bias, male or female.

Group List   An electronic roster of e-mail addresses.

Hacker   A technically adept individual who accesses or manipulates corporate and individual computer systems. Malicious hackers, like crackers and computer criminals, are intent on causing damage. Nonmalicious hackers are motivated by a sense of challenge or curiosity.

Hardware   Physical computer system components.

Hidden Reader   An unintended e-mail reader.

Imperative Mood   Expresses a command. For example: "Department heads: Alert your staffs to the dangers of sending inappropriate e-mail messages."

Inbox   The place where received e-mail messages are stored.

Intended Reader   The person(s) to whom an e-mail writer addresses and sends a message.

Internet   A worldwide collection of computer networks. Home to the World Wide Web. Synonymous with the Net.

Internet downloading   Software piracy extends to the Internet. While it may be easy, it also is illegal to download copyrighted software from the Internet or bulletin boards without permission from the software copyright owner.

Inverted Pyramid   The writing approach favored by journalists. The most important information or conclusion comes first, followed by information in descending order of importance.

Jargon   Technical language, or slang, unfamiliar to general readers.

Lead   The first sentence(s) of the first paragraph.

Listserv   Generic term for mail-handling software that lets people subscribe and unsubscribe to electronic mailing lists.[7]

Malicious Hackers   Cybervandals and cyberthieves who crash systems to steal passwords, trade secrets, and other valuable data, costing users enormous amounts of time and money.

Message   A single e-mail communication, generally limited to one page.

Net Synonymous with the Internet. A worldwide network of computers communicating in a common language via telephone lines or microwave links. Home of the World Wide Web.

Netiquette E-mail etiquette. The dos and don'ts of cyberspace.

Network A hardware and/or software combination that connects two or more computers and enables them to share and/or transfer data.

Network Administrator Person responsible for operating and maintaining a computer network.

Passive Voice The subject of the verb is the receiver, not the doer, of the action. Example: The off-color e-mail message (object) was sent by the bitter ex-employee (subject as passive receiver) upon her termination.

Priority Designates an e-mail message's importance as high, normal, or low. Gives the reader an indication of how quickly the message should be opened and acted upon.

Recipient The receiver, or reader, of an e-mail message. Recipients include intended and hidden, or unintended, readers.

Redundant Modifier A word that means the same thing as the word it modifies. For example, *completely dead, absolutely certain, totally full.*

Redundant Pairs Words that are commonly paired for no good reason. Examples: *each and every, here and now, one and only.*

Renting The illegal practice of renting software without permission of the copyright holder.

Reply The response to an e-mail message.

Salutation The greeting that appears at the beginning of an e-mail message.

Sexist Language Indicates a male or female bias.

Shareware   Software that is passed out freely for evaluation purposes only. The evaluation period is typically 30 days.[8]

Signature   A personal identifier that appears at the end of an e-mail message. May include the writer's name, company name, street address, phone number, and a hyperlink to the organization's Web site.

Signature File   A predefined signature that can be inserted at the end of an e-mail message.

Smileys   Electronic symbols of emotion, also called "emoticons." For example, the symbol :) indicates the writer is smiling.

Snail Mail   Using the postal service to mail letters the good old-fashioned way.

Social Engineering   When hackers use human error to their benefit. It could involve a hacker talking an employee out of a password. Or it could be dumpster diving, rooting through trash containers for information to enable the hacker to crack the organization's computer system.

Softlifting   In the workplace, softlifting occurs when extra copies of software are made for employees to take home, and/or extra copies are made for the office. If you purchase software with a single-user license, then load it on multiple computers or servers, you are guilty of "softloading."[9]

Software   Computer programs, such as those for e-mail or word processing.

Software Piracy   The unauthorized use of software.

Spam   Unsolicited electronic junk mail.

Spell checker   The computer application that checks a document's spelling.

Spoofing   Faking e-mail addresses and Web pages to get users to reveal passwords, credit card information, or other critical data.

Subject Line   The topic of an e-mail message.

Traditional Correspondence   Nonelectronic writing.

Unbundling   Separating software from the products with which it was intended to be bundled or sold. Unscrupulous software distributors sometimes sell at a discount software that has been unbundled. If a deal seems too good to be true, it probably is.[10]

Virus   An infectious computer bug that it typically spread through e-mail attachments and illegal, unlicensed software. Symptoms range from mild to deadly.

Warez   Pirated or illegal software. In general, the standard in the Internet community is to make plural words describing illegal activity using the letter z instead of s. Software or sites labeled as warz usually contain illegal material and should be avoided and reported.[11]

Webzine   A Web site that publishes original content.

Work Station Computer   The computer that sits atop an employee's desk. A desktop computer.

World Wide Web (www)   A global online information source of interconnected data. Also called the Web.

Zine   A small, inexpensive, self-published, online document.

Resources and Expert Sources

E-Policy Development, Implementation, and Training
E-Policy Institute™
Nancy Flynn, Managing Director
2300 Walhaven Ct., Suite 200A
Columbus, OH 43220
800/292-7332
614/451-8701
www.epolicyinstitute.com

E-Communications, E-Writing, and Netiquette Training
E-Policy Institute™
Nancy Flynn, Managing Director
2300 Walhaven Ct., Suite 200A
Columbus, OH 43220
800/292-7332
614/451-8701
www.epolicyinstitute.com

Cyberinsurance
Assurex International
445 Hutchinson Avenue
Columbus, OH 43235-1408
614/888-4869
www.assurex.com

Cyberlaw

Bricker & Eckler LLP
Mark C. Pomeroy, Partner
100 S. Third St.
Columbus, OH 43215
614/227-2300
www.bricker.com

Carlile Patchen & Murphy, LLP
Marie-Joëlle C. Khouzam, Attorney
366 East Broad Street
Columbus, OH 43215
614/228-6135
www.cpmlaw.com

Fair Measures Corporation
Rita Risser, Attorney
PO Box 2146
Santa Cruz, CA 95063
831/458-0500
www.fairmeasures.com

Lane, Alton & Horst, Attorneys at Law
Donald C. Slowik, Esq.
Christopher T. O'Shaughnessy, Esq.
175 S. Third St.
Columbus, OH 43215
614/228-6885
www.lane@lah4law.com

E-Risk Management and Computer Forensics

Computer Forensics Inc.™
Joan E. Feldman, President
1749 Dexter Ave. N
Seattle, WA 98109
206/324-6232
www.forensics.com

E-Risk Management/Computer Security/Hacker-Cracker Insurance
INSUREtrust.com
Steven H. Haase, CEO
1100 Johnson Ferry Road NE, Suite 900
Atlanta, GA 30342
770/200-8000
www.INSUREtrust.com

Software Piracy
Software & Information Industry Association (SIIA)
SPA Anti-Piracy Division
1730 M. Street NW, Suite 700
Washington, DC 20036
800/388-7478 (piracy hot line)
www.siia.net/piracy (piracy hot line)

Business Software Alliance (BSA)
1150 18th Street NW, Suite 700
Washington, DC 20036
888/667-4722 (piracy hot line)
www.bsa.org

Suggested Reading

E-Communication and E-Policy Development

Flynn, Nancy and Tom Flynn, *Writing Effective E-Mail: Improving Your Electronic Communication*. Menlo, Park, CA: Crisp Publications, Inc., 1998.

Hale, Constance, ed., *Wired Style: Principles of English Usage in the Digital Age*. San Francisco, CA: HardWired, 1996.

Hartman, Diane B. and Karen S. Nantz, *The 3 Rs of E-Mail: Risks, Rights, and Responsibilities*. Menlo Park, CA: Crisp Publications, Inc., 1996.

Overly, Michael R., *E-Policy: How to Develop Computer, E-mail and Internet Guidelines to Protect Your Company and Its Assets*. New York, NY: AMACOM, 1999.

Smedinghoff, Thomas J., ed., *Online Law: The SPA's Legal Guide to Doing Business on the Internet*. Reading, MA: Addison-Wesley Developers Press, 1996.

Writing Style Manuals and Writing Policy Development

Corbett, Edward, P. J., *The Little English Handbook: Choices and Conventions*. New York, NY: John Wiley & Sons, 1977.

Skillin, Marjorie E., Robert M. Gay, et al., *Words into Type*, 3d ed. Upper Saddle River, NJ: Prentice Hall, 1974.

Tarshis, Barry, *Grammar for Smart People*. New York, NY: Pocket Books, 1992.

The University of Chicago, *The Chicago Manual of Style*, 14th ed. Chicago, IL: The University of Chicago Press, 1993.

Williams, Joseph, M., *Style: Ten Lessons in Clarity & Grace*. Glenview, Il.: Scott, Foresman and Company, 1981.

NOTES

Introduction

1. Science & Ideas, *U.S. News & World Report*, March 22, 1999, 60.

2. *USA Today*, March 1999.

3. Joseph McCafferty, "The Phantom Menace," *CFO*, June 1999, 90-91.

4. Keith Naughton, "CyberSlacking," *Newsweek*, November 29, 1999, 63.

5. Barbara Carmen, "Fire Division Caught Peeking at Porno-graphic Sites on the Internet," *The Columbus Dispatch*, August 1, 1999.

6. Keith Naughton, "CyberSlacking," *Newsweek*, November 29, 1999, 64.

7. Richard Power, "1999 CSI/FBI Computer Crime and Security Survey," *Computer Security Issues & Trends*, vol. V, no. 1, Winter 1999, 7.

8. Ann Carrns, "Prying Times: Those Bawdy E-Mails Were Good for a Laugh Until the Ax Fell," *The Wall Street Journal*, February 4, 2000, A8, col. 1

9. *Ibid.*, A1, col. 1.

10. Software & Information Industry Association, *SIIA's Report on Global Software Piracy 2000* (Washington, DC: Software & Information Industry Association, © 2000).

11. Richard Power, "1999 CSI/FBI Computer Crime and Security Survey," *Computer Security Issues & Trends*, vol. V, no. 1, Winter 1999, 7.

12. L. Nicholson, "Oops, Wrong E-Mail Address List. A Dirty Joke Goes Global," *Philadelphia Inquirer*, May 8, 1999.

13. Richard Power, "2000 CSI/FBI Computer Crime and Security Survey," *Computer Security Issues & Trends*, vol. VI, no. 1, Spring 2000, 4.

14. Cover Story, "CyberCrime," *Business Week*, February 21, 2000, 38.

15. Keith Naughton, "CyberSlacking," *Newsweek*, November 29, 1999, 65.

Chapter 1

1. Benjamin Lowe, "Companies Taking E-Commerce to Next Level Using Internet," *The Columbus Dispatch*, December 13, 1999, business sec., 8-9.

2. Anne R. Carey and Quin Tian, "USA Snapshots®," *USA Today*, October 19, 1999, 1D.

Chapter 3

1. The cyberlaw information contained in Chapter 3 is based on interviews with Joan Feldman, president of Computer Forensics Inc.™, as well as attorneys Mark Pomeroy, Bricker & Eckler LLP; Rita Risser, Fair Measures Corporation; Dan Langin, InsureTrust.com; and Donald Slowik, Lane, Alton & Horst.

2. American Management Association, *2000 AMA Survey: Workplace Monitoring & Surveillance* (New York: American Management Association, © 2000).

3. James T. Harrison, "Managing the Electronic Workplace: E-mail and the Internet," *Resources*, Spring 2000, 6.

4. Excerpted from "Voice Mail and Computer Access Policy," © 2000 prepared by Attorney Marie-Joëlle C. Khouzam, Carlile Patchen & Murphy, LLP. For informational purposes only. No reliance should be placed on this without the advice of counsel.

5. Excerpted from "Computer Network and the Internet Acceptable Use Policy." © 1997-2000, Bricker & Eckler LLP. All rights reserved. Prepared by Attorney Mark C. Pomeroy. For informational purposes only. No reliance should be placed on this without advice of counsel.

6. Excerpted from "Internet and E-Mail Policy." Copyright 2000, Fair Measures Corporation, used with permission. For an updated policy, go to www.FairMeasures.com.

7. *Ibid.*

8. Excerpted from "Computer Network and the Internet Acceptable Use Policy." © 1997-2000, Bricker & Eckler LLP. All rights reserved. Prepared by Attorney Mark C. Pomeroy. For informational purposes only. No reliance should be placed on this without advice of counsel.

9. Excerpted from "Internet and E-Mail Policy." Copyright 2000, Fair Measures Corporation, used with permission. For an updated policy, go to www.FairMeasures.com.

10. Excerpted from "Computer Network and the Internet Acceptable Use Policy." © 1997-2000, Bricker & Eckler LLP. All rights reserved. Prepared by Attorney Mark C. Pomeroy. For informational purposes only. No reliance should be placed on this without advice of counsel.

11. Excerpted from "Internet and E-Mail Policy." Copyright 2000, Fair Measures Corporation, used with permission. For an updated policy, go to www.FairMeasures.com.

12. Richard Power, "2000 CSI/FBI Computer Crime and Security Survey," *Computer Security Issues & Trends*, vol. VI, no. 1, Spring 2000, 7.

13. Excerpted from "Internet and E-Mail Policy." Copyright 2000, Fair Measures Corporation, used with permission. For an updated policy, go to www.FairMeasures.com.

14. Excerpted from "Computer Network and the Internet Acceptable Use Policy." © 1997-2000, Bricker & Eckler LLP. All rights reserved. Prepared by Attorney Mark C. Pomeroy. For informational purposes only. No reliance should be placed on this without advice of counsel.

15. *Ibid.*

16. *Ibid.*

17. Excerpted from "Internet and E-Mail Policy." Copyright 2000, Fair Measures Corporation, used with permission. For an updated policy, go to www.FairMeasures.com.

Chapter 4

1. The e-risk management information and tips in Chapter 4 are based on interviews by the author with Joan E. Feldman, president, Computer Forensics Inc.™; Tom Flynn, co-author, *Writing Effective E-Mail: Improving Your Electronic Communication*; and Steven H. Hasse, president, and William Corbitt, vice president, technical assessment and loss control, INSUREtrust.com.

2. Philip Pierson, "E-Commerce: A New World with New Risks," (Presentation to Roach, Howard, Smith & Hunter, Inc., June 1999), 2.

3. Richard B. Schmitt, "The Cybersuit: How Computers Aided Lawyers in Diet-Pill Case," *The Wall Street Journal*, October 8, 1999, B1.

4. Excerpted from "Use of E-Mail, Network, and Internet/Intranet Policy." © 2000, Donald C. Slowik, Attorney at Law with Lane, Alton, & Horst. For informational purposes only. Individual policies should be developed with assistance from competent legal counsel.

5. Cindy Hall and Marcy E. Mullins, "USA Snapshots®," *USA Today*, March 28, 2000, 1D.

6. Based on an interview with the author and Joan Feldman, president, Computer Forensics Inc.™

7. Excerpted from "Internet and E-Mail Policy." Copyright 2000, Fair Measures Corporation, used with permission. For an updated policy, go to www.FairMeasures.com."

8. Michael J. McCarthy, "You Assumed 'Erase' Wiped Out That Rant Against the Boss? Nope," *The Wall Street Journal*, March 7, 2000, A16.

Chapter 5

1. Richard Power, "2000 CSI/FBI Computer Crime and Security Survey," *Computer Security Issues & Trends*, vol. VI, no. 1, Spring 2000, 4.

2. Richard Power, "1999 CSI/FBI Computer Crime and Security Survey," *Computer Security Issues & Trends*, vol. V., no. 1, Winter 1999, 4-5.

3. Richard Power, "2000 CSI/FBI Computer Crime and Security Survey," *Computer Security Issues & Trends*, vol. VI, no. 1, Spring 2000, 5.

4. The computer security tips in Chapter 5 are based on interviews by the author with Steven H. Haase, president, and William Corbitt, vice president of technical assessment and loss control, INSUREtrust.com; Joan E. Feldman, president, Computer Forensics Inc.™; and Tom Flynn, coauthor of *Writing Effective E-Mail: Improving Your Electronic Communication.*

5. Richard Power, "1999 CSI/FBI Computer Crime and Security Survey," *Computer Security Issues & Trends,* vol. v, no. 1, Winter 1999, 6.

6. Cover Story, "CyberCrime," *Business Week,* February 21, 2000, 39.

7. *Ibid.*

8. Richard Power, "2000 CSI/FBI Computer Crime and Security Survey," Computer Security Issues & Trends, vol. VI, no. 1, Spring 2000, page 7.

9. *Ibid.*

Chapter 6

1. The cyberinsurance product information and tips in Chapter 6 are based on interviews by the author with Assurex International President and CEO Thomas W. Harvey and Assurex Partners Andy Barrengos and Steve Sawyer, Woodruff-Sawyer & Co.; Brooke Hunter, Hunter, Keilty, Muntz & Beatty; Gary Kloehn, Barney & Barney LLC; David Kohl, Roach Howard Smith & Hunter; Vernon O'Neal, Hamilton Dorsey Alston Company; and Ronald Wanglin, Bolton & Co. Additional interviews were conducted with Steven H. Hasse, William Corbitt, and Dan Langin of INSUREtrust.com.

Chapter 8

1. The tips on avoiding and using e-mail, as well as the attachment guidelines in Chapter 8, include material excerpted from the author's previous book: Nancy Flynn and Tom Flynn, *Writing Effec-*

tive E-Mail: Improving Your Electronic Communication (Menlo Park, CA: Crisp Publications, © 1998).

Chapter 9

1. Netiquette guidelines include material excerpted from the author's previous book: Nancy Flynn and Tom Flynn, *Writing Effective E-Mail: Improving Your Electronic Communication* (Menlo Park, CA: Crisp Publications, © 1998).

Chapter 11

1. The software piracy discussion in Chapter 11 is based on written material provided by the SPA Anti-Piracy Division of the Software & Information Industry Association (SIIA). For more information about software piracy, visit SIIA online at www.siia.net.

2. Software & Information Industry Association, *SIIA's Report on Global Software Piracy 1999* (Washington, DC: Software & Information Industry Association, © 1999).

3. Software & Information Industry Association, *SIIA's Report on Global Software Piracy 2000* (Washington, DC: Software & Information Industry Association, © 2000).

4. Business Software Alliance, "Columbus-Area Firm Settles Software Piracy Claim: Mortgage Company Pays Software Watchdog Group $139,000" (Washington, DC: Business Software Alliance press release, November 3, 1999).

5. Software & Information Industry Association, www.siia.net/ programs/backgrounder.htm (Washington, DC: Software & Information Industry Association, 2000).

6. *Ibid.*

7. Software usage checklist includes material excerpted from the Software & Information Industry Association's Web site (www.siia.net).

8. Software & Information Industry Association, www.siia.net/
piracy/programs/q&a.htm (Washington, DC: Software & Information Industry Association, 2000).

Chapter 13

1. Chapter 13's discussion of subject lines, leads, and the inverted pyramid writing style includes material excerpted from the author's previous book: Nancy Flynn and Tom Flynn, *Writing Effective E-Mail: Improving Your Electronic Communication* (Menlo Park, CA: Crisp Publications, © 1998).

Chapter 14

1. Chapter 14 includes material (electronic spelling tips, active voice, power versus puny words, appropriate tone, and the five Ws) excerpted from the author's previous book: Nancy Flynn and Tom Flynn, *Writing Effective E-Mail: Improving Your Electronic Communication* (Menlo Park, CA: Crisp Publications, © 1998).

Chapter 15

1. Chapter 15 includes material (using conversational language, bending a few rules, avoiding sexist language, avoiding e-communication pitfalls, communicating with international readers, the language of electronic abbreviations, lists of acronyms and smileys) excerpted from the author's previous book: Nancy Flynn and Tom Flynn, *Writing Effective E-Mail: Improving Your Electronic Communication* (Menlo Park, CA: Crisp Publications, © 1998).

Chapter 16

1. The e-mail formatting guidelines section includes material (creating visual emphasis and emphasizing electronic text) excerpted from the author's previous book: Nancy Flynn and Tom Flynn, *Writing Effective E-Mail: Improving Your Electronic Communication* (Menlo Park, CA: Crisp Publications, © 1998).

Chapter 19

1. Gregory Vistica, "Inside the Secret Cyberwar," *Newsweek*, February 21, 2000, 48.

Appendix B

1. Donald S. Skupsky, JD, CRM, "Legal and Operational Definitions of a Record," *Records Management Quarterly*, (January 1995), p. 39.

Appendix D

1. The author is grateful to Crisp Publications for granting permission to incorporate glossary material from her previous book. Nancy and Tom Fynn, *Writing Effective E-Mail: Improving Your Electronic Communication* (Menlo Park, CA: Crisp Publications, © 1998.

2. Thomas J. Smedinghoff, ed., *Online Law: The SPA's Legal Guide to Doing Business on the Internet* (Reading, MA: Addison-Wesley Developers Press, 1996), 510.

3. Software & Information Industry Association, *www.siia.net/piracy* (Washington, DC: Software & Information Industry Association, 2000).

4. *Ibid.*

5. Constance Hale, ed., *Wired Style: Principles of English Usage in the Digital Age* (San Francisco, CA: HardWired, 1996), 55.

6. Software & Information Industry Association, *www.siia.net/piracy/programs/share* (Washington, DC: Software & Information Industry Association, 2000).

7. Constance Hale, ed., *Wired Style: Principles of English Usage in the Digital Age* (San Francisco, CA: HardWired, 1996), 152.

8. Software & Information Industry Association, *www.siia.net/piracy* (Washington, DC: Software & Information Industry Association, 2000).

9. *Ibid.*

10. *Ibid.*

11. *Ibid.*

Index

About the Author

Nancy Flynn is founder and managing director of the E-Policy Institute™, an organization devoted to helping employers limit e-risks through the development and implementation of effective e-mail, Internet, and software policies. Through the E-Policy Institute, she conducts e-policy seminars, netiquette programs, and electronic writing workshops for corporations, associations, and government entities nationwide. In addition, the E-Policy Institute offers a full range of e-policy products and training tools to help limit e-risks and reduce liability costs. When she is not busy training and speaking, Ms. Flynn works individually with clients as a consultant, business writer, and corporate writing coach.

Recognized for her expertise in the areas of e-policy development and electronic communication, Flynn has been featured in *The Wall Street Journal, Woman's Day*, the Associated Press, and National Public Radio, among other national media outlets.

Flynn is coauthor of *Writing Effective E-Mail: Improving Your Electronic Communication* and author of *The $100,000 Writer: How to Make a Six-Figure Income as a Freelance Business Writer*.

You may visit the E-Policy Institute online at www.epolicy institute.com, or contact Nancy Flynn directly via phone, fax, or snail mail.

Nancy Flynn, Managing Director
E-Policy Institute™
2300 Walhaven Ct., Suite 200A
Columbus, OH 43220
800/292-7332 phone
614/451-8726 fax
www.epolicyinstitute.com